Sirens & Sinners

Hans Helmut Prinzler

Sirens & Sinners

A Visual History
of Weimar Film
1918–1933

with 443 illustrations, 335 in duotone

Thames & Hudson

Translated from the German by David H. Wilson

First published in the United Kingdom in 2013 by
Thames & Hudson Ltd, 181A High Holborn, London WC1V 7QX

www.thamesandhudson.com

First published in 2013 in hardcover in the United States of America by
Thames & Hudson Inc., 500 Fifth Avenue, New York, New York 10110

thamesandhudsonusa.com

Authorized English-language edition of *Licht und Schatten.*
Die grossen Stumm- und Tonfilme der Weimarer Republik.
355 Filmbilder von Mutter Krause bis Dr. Mabuse
originally published in 2012 by Schirmer/Mosel, Munich
in collaboration with Deutsche Kinemathek, Berlin
and Friedrich-Wilhelm-Murnau-Stiftung, Wiesbaden.

Original edition copyright © 2012 Schirmer/Mosel, Munich
German text copyright © 2012 Hans Helmut Prinzler
This edition copyright © 2013 Thames & Hudson Ltd, London

British Library Cataloguing-in-Publication Data
A catalogue record for this book is available from the British Library

Library of Congress Catalog Card Number 2012955178

ISBN: 978-0-500-51689-8

Printed and bound in Italy

Contents

Foreword

The purpose of stills photography has always been to create publicity for films. Production companies pass these images on to the press and the cinemas in the hope that they will entice customers to the box office. If the film is a comedy, the image needs to be funny; if it's science fiction, the choice will most likely be some vision of the future; if it's a murder mystery or a thriller, there will be shadowy figures or faces rigid with fear. What these images show are typical scenes, a particular atmosphere or the stars of the show.

Even in the earliest days of cinema, stills were also given to graphic artists, who used them to design the first film posters; later they would also create illustrations of dramatic scenes, which they combined with fancy type or hand-lettering denoting the title of the film, the actors and the production company. The more abstract and individualistic the design, the more the poster itself became a work of art. There were also combinations of photography and illustration, photomontages, and photographs used alone, but it was stills that provided the basic building blocks.

Stills capture characteristic scenes from the film, ideally just as they appear on screen. In the Asta Nielsen picture *The Film Primadonna* (1913), directed by Urban Gad, we are actually shown how stills are shot: after the actors have been filmed sitting on a bench, the cameraman switches to a stills camera, the actors pose motionless on the bench, and the still is taken. Even in the 1920s, however, it was unusual for the film cameraman to take the stills as well. Heinrich Gärtner, who worked as a cameraman mainly for Richard Eichberg productions, always put a stamp on the back of his stills: 'Every copy should be marked – photograph by H. Gärtner.'

Generally, photographers were hired to take the stills, as it was a specialist job in itself. It was not, however, highly regarded by the filmmakers or even by the photographers themselves, but some practitioners took it very seriously, and opened their own studios for portrait photography. Film stars and other big names in the industry would go to these 'real' studios to have their portraits taken, and in Hollywood the big film companies even had special photography studios on their lots, where the images of the stars and the whole publicity machine for each production would be carefully put together. In Germany, only Ufa (Universum-Film AG) had a small photography studio of this kind. In the mid-1920s, Erich Pommer hired the photographer Hans Natge to work on the film *The Ancient Law* (1923, directed by Ewald André Dupont), and he used a technique that he called *Momentfotografie*, i.e. he took pictures while the film shoot was in progress and not afterwards. This method was also recorded on film: in the fragment *Der Film im Film*

[*The Film Within the Film*] (1923–24), directed by Friedrich Porges, we can actually see Natge at work, standing next to the cameraman on a platform during the filming of *The Ancient Law*. Natge shot stills for a number of Ufa films: *A Waltz-Dream* (1925), directed by Ludwig Berger, *The Last Laugh* (1924), directed by F. W. Murnau, *Variety* (1925), directed by E. A. Dupont, *Faust* (1925–26), directed by F. W. Murnau, and *Manon Lescaut* (1925–26), directed by Arthur Robison. His technique did not catch on, however, as the producers found it too expensive – stills were not meant to cost so much.

Occasionally, illustrated magazines would send well-known photographers such as Mario von Bucovich or Laszlo Willinger along to the film studios to report on how the camera team worked, or how the director staged a scene, or how the stars were made up. These working photographs of the production process were sometimes staged so that the famous photographer could put his subject matter together in as short a time as possible for a mass-circulation magazine. Stills photographers also took working photographs – as mementoes, out of interest, or on commission. Depending on the client's wishes, between 400 and 800 stills would be shot per film, and ten per cent of these would be working photographs.

On most days, the main task of the stills photographer was to wait. He had to wait until the actors had been made up, the scene had been lit and shot, and the director had given his instructions and expressed his satisfaction with the take. After that, the photographer had to grab the actors, or fetch them back from wherever they had disappeared to, and get them to pose as if they were acting the same scene. Would the director have been bothered about the quality of the still? Would the cameraman have ceded his vantage point to the photographer? It's easy to imagine that every day at the studio would have been a new battle because, when all was said and done, the stills photographer was an afterthought and an irritation to all concerned.

The names of very few of these photographers have survived from the days of the Weimar Republic. Names such as Horst von Harbou and Hans Casparius cannot be found in the advertisements or lists of professional associations, and the provenance of many of the images themselves is unknown because the photographers rarely put their stamp on them. In 1929, a book was published entitled *1200 interessante Photos aus den besten Filmen aller Länder* [*1,200 Interesting Photos from the Best Films from all Countries*], but not one of the photographers is named.

The specialist book *Der kleine Aufnahmeleiter* [*The Little Production Manager*] (1927 edition) names thirteen stars but only seven photographers, including Walter Lichtenstein, who later during his exile in France became famous under the name 'Limot', Karl Lindner from Neukölln, and Alexander Schmoll, who always stamped his pictures.

Can stills photography be called an art form? Perhaps we should leave that question to those who continue to debate whether film itself can be called an art. What is beyond doubt is that they remain much in demand.

Museums all over the world borrow them from the Deutsche Kinemathek, and original stills from films made during the Weimar Republic are always in high demand. Prints of the classics from the collection fetch high prices at auction. The archives of the Deutsche Kinemathek contain some 30,000 images from this period. The following pages present many high-quality photographs that provide an impressive record of some famous movies and of others that are lesser known or have even faded into oblivion.

This book invites its readers to travel back to this fascinating period in the history of German cinema, and reminds us how little we know about this long undervalued art form.

Rainer Rother and Werner Sudendorf
Deutsche Kinemathek, Berlin

The Restless Republic
New Directions in Germany 1918–33

Hans Helmut Prinzler

Weimar: a city in the state of Thuringia with a long cultural tradition; a place of symbolic significance for the whole of Germany. Republic: a democratic form of state; perhaps the best of all forms. The time: 1918 to 1933. This was one of the most creative periods in the history of the German cinema.

It is a history that is often divided into political periods: Imperial, Weimar Republic, Nazi, postwar, East and West German, post-Unification. To a far greater extent than in Great Britain, France or the US, the different forms of national government exercised a profound influence on German cinema. Other countries prefer to divide history into decades, but in Germany that tends to have been the case only since the 1950s. There was also a short overlap between the Weimar Republic and National Socialism.

The Weimar Republic, named after the town in which its constitution was drawn up, lasted for fourteen years, three months and fifteen days if we define it by two key dates: it began on 9 November 1918 with the proclamation by the Social Democrat Philipp Scheidemann, and ended on 23 March 1933, when the 'Enabling Act' to suspend the Weimar Constitution was passed in the Reichstag.

The first German republic had its own shades of light and dark. The light shone mainly on art and culture. The dark side included political instability, the rise of Nazism and the perilous economic situation. With hindsight, the period can be viewed from many different perspectives. Subjectively and artistically, it has been called a golden age; objectively and historically, it saw the end of a democracy.

Politics

In November 1918, the war came to an end, and suddenly the Germans were without a Kaiser. The armistice and the abdication of Wilhelm II brought no stability; the mood was revolutionary but confused. In Berlin and other large cities, workers and military councils agitated for new structures, but the less radical initiatives taken by the people's councils met with greater success, and helped to establish a civic, parliamentary state governed by a constitution. In August 1919, the German National Assembly in Weimar laid the basis for this, the first German republic, based on the principle of a representative democracy divided into the legislature (the Reichstag), the executive (president and government) and the judiciary. The new constitution granted individual human rights, to a large extent guaranteed equality before the law, and declared it to be the fundamental duty of every German 'to use his mental and physical powers for the benefit of the community'. Today this sounds well tailored to fit the historical situation of the time, but the language

Friedrich Ebert and Paul von Hindenburg.

of the constitution did not correspond to the aggressive realities of the political situation.

The unreasonable demands imposed by the Treaty of Versailles (June 1919), attempted coups from both left and right, the vacillations of the politicians and the progressive deterioration of the economy all determined the predominantly negative mood of the first five years. By the mid-1920s, Gustav Stresemann's foreign policies brought more stability, and also helped to calm things down at home, but the governing coalitions were always fragile and never completed a full term of office.

Two presidents of the Reich left their mark on the period: the Social Democrat Friedrich Ebert (1871–1925), who held the office for six years, and Paul von Hindenburg (1847–1934), who was in power for eight. But between 1919 and 1933, there were no less than fourteen different Chancellors. With the death of Stresemann (1929), the world economic crisis and a never-ending sequence of elections, the political situation became increasingly complicated, ultimately leading to the worst possible outcome: the seizure of power by the Nazis.

At its peak, the Weimar Republic consisted of eighteen *Länder* or regions. The smallest was the Free State of Schaumburg-Lippe, with 48,000 inhabitants (capital: Bückeburg), and the largest was Prussia, with 38 million inhabitants (capital: Berlin). Prussia extended to the west as far as the Rhineland, and to the east as far as Königsberg. Each *Land* had its own politico-cultural role to play in the spheres of theatre, music, art and culture. As far as the cinema was concerned, the political focus lay not on support for or promotion of the medium, but on protecting young people, dictating what did or did not constitute entertainment, and direct censorship. On the other hand, politicians liked to be seen at premieres, especially when the film starred anyone famous. President Friedrich Ebert's visit to the set during the filming of *Anne Boleyn* in September 1920 went down in history. Ernst Lubitsch was the director, the film starred Emil Jannings and Henny Porten, and according to contemporary accounts Lubitsch had a great deal of trouble controlling the 4,000 extras – most of them unemployed – during the wedding procession. Also on record is the attendance of Chancellor Wilhelm Marx, Foreign Minister Gustav Stresemann, and Reichsbank president Hjalmar Schacht at the premiere of F. W. Murnau's *Faust* in October 1926 at the Ufa Palast am Zoo in Berlin. By then, the director had already left for America.

Censorship

In November 1918, censorship in Germany – including that of films, which had previously been carried out by the police as a means of preserving 'public peace, security and order' – was abolished. The new freedom resulted in a few so-called 'educational' (i.e. sexually explicit) films that appeared to be morally somewhat dubious, and so in April 1920, the National Assembly passed the *Reichslichtspielgesetz* or Reich Cinema Law, setting up offices in

Berlin and Munich to examine films before distribution. Controversial cases usually concerned moral standards in the depiction of sexuality, and less frequently political issues. Generally, children were banned from seeing such films. There was much discussion of the bans imposed on the following films: *Vorderhaus und Hinterhaus* [*Front Door and Back Door*] by Richard Oswald, *White Slave Traffic* by Jaap Speyer, *Gesetze der Liebe* [*Laws of Love*] by Magnus Hirschfeld and Richard Oswald, *§ 182 Minderjährig* [*Paragraph 182 Minors*] by Ernst Winar, *Sex in Chains* by Wilhelm Dieterle, *Adieu Mascotte* by Wilhelm Thiele, *Cyankali* by Hans Tintner, and *Whither Germany?* (p. 270) by Slatan Dudow. In the majority of cases, prolonged negotiations, sometimes followed by cuts, resulted in the overall ban being commuted to the exclusion of children. Two of the most spectacular bans on foreign films were those imposed on Sergei Eisenstein's *Battleship Potemkin* and Lewis Milestone's *All Quiet on the Western Front*. The ban on the latter film, based on the novel by Erich Maria Remarque, followed systematic interference by the Nazis. From 1933 onwards, the new authorities imposed rigid state censorship on everything.

The Economy

War costs a lot of money, and a lost war inevitably leads to a prolonged economic crisis. In Germany, the traumatic consequences of the First World War included an often frightening struggle for day-to-day existence, and substantial financial losses, especially among the middle classes. The once stable gold mark had already been replaced by paper money in 1914, and the war itself cost Germany over 198 million gold marks. Disputes over the amount of money to be paid for reparations went on for years. Since these national debts could not be paid through normal financial measures, the first major breakdown came with hyperinflation in November 1923. Attempts to stabilize the economy had lasted for barely six years when in autumn 1929 the country was again plunged into economic darkness by the Wall Street Crash in the US. In Germany, the worst effects were felt in the labour market, with unemployment rising from 1.4 million in 1929 to 5 million by the end of 1930, then to a peak of 6.1 million in February 1932. Cuts in social services led to widespread protests, and resulted in substantial support for the National Socialist Party because, unlike all the other parties, it made populist promises that greatly appealed to the masses.

The Economics of Film

For culture in general and for the cinema in particular, the financial side of things played a major role in two respects: production and consumption. The making and the distribution of films were both extremely expensive, but the public also had to be able to afford to go to the cinema. Sets, costumes and the stars themselves demanded large-scale investments, but the public would come only if they felt it would be worth the effort. During the Weimar Republic, German films were held in relatively high esteem in Germany, with only American films exceeding them in popularity. For the first half of the 1920s there are no reliable statistics concerning cinema audiences, but the number of German films and cinemas from 1919 onwards and audience figures from 1926 to 1933 are extremely revealing:

Year	Films	Cinemas	Audiences
1919	770	2,836	?
1921	240	3,647	?
1923	253	2,700	?
1925	212	3,878	?
1926	185	4,293	332 million
1927	242	4,462	337 million
1928	224	5,267	353 million
1929	183	5,073	328 million
1930	146	5,059	290 million
1931	144	5,066	273 million
1932	132	5,059	238 million
1933	114	5,071	245 million

It should be remembered that 1923 was the year of hyperinflation, 1929 the world economic crisis, and 1929–30 the time when silent films gave way to sound. Statistically, 1927–28 were the peak years.

Technology

One characteristic feature of the Weimar Republic was the number of inventions and technological advances that had a direct effect on communications and communal life. The speed of life accelerated, especially in the big cities. The motor car industry took a huge step forward when Opel introduced mass production, and Berlin constructed the AVUS, the first controlled-access highway, which was also used as a racing track. This period saw the first automatic dialling telephones, and the radio was already on its way to becoming a cultural mass medium. The airship *Graf Zeppelin* flew from Germany to the US in 1928, and a year later flew around the world. German technologists and engineers played a leading role in many inventions and new developments.

Talking Pictures

The switch from silent movies to talkies was another advance in which Germany played a crucial role. In 1919, Josef Engl, Joseph Massolle and Hans Vogt patented a technique in which sound was recorded directly onto a film print and then read by the projector. At the time, the industry failed to recognize the importance of this invention, and the patents were sold to Switzerland, where a US company acquired the licence. When the US film industry found itself facing a major crisis in 1926, different sound techniques were tested, and this German 'Tri-Ergon' system outshone all its competitors. In Germany, AEG, Siemens and Telefunken developed a similar technique, and the joint foundation of a company called Klangfilm ('Sound Film'), which also produced the appropriate projection equipment, set the talkie on the road to its eventual triumph. The first German film to use sound all the way through was *Melody of the World* (1929), an experimental film by Walther Ruttmann.

The economic consequences were wide-ranging. Many producers and cinema owners were unable to attract enough investment and went bankrupt, while the international circulation of films initially stagnated, because it was far more difficult to dub films than to translate the intertitles into the appropriate language. On the other hand, the public were eager to see talking pictures. It took the German film industry two years to make the transition from silent film to sound.

Sport

In sport too, the 1920s can be regarded as a golden era. There was a large increase in the number of sports clubs (both middle- and working-class) and in the number of sports played. Until then, football had been regarded as un-German and uncouth, but now it gained mass appeal, both on the field and in the stands of large stadiums. Motor racing also drew big crowds, competitive cycling became popular, and Max Schmeling made boxing – which was banned throughout the Reich – into a national sport, albeit for spectators and on the radio rather than actively in the ring. In 1927, Schmeling became light-heavyweight champion of Europe, and the fight, which took place in Dortmund, was the first to be broadcast live on German radio. Several million avid boxing fans tuned in. In 1928, Schmeling moved up to the heavyweight division, and in 1930 he became world champion.

Max Schmeling in the boxing ring.

Sport on Film

Max Schmeling was a link between sport and cinema not only because of his marriage to actress Anny Ondra, but also because in 1930 he played the leading role in the boxing film *Liebe im Ring* [*Love in the Ring*], co-starring with Renate Müller. The first two German feature films about football were made in 1927: *Die elf Teufel* [*The Eleven Devils*] starred Gustav Fröhlich as a centre-forward who is poached by a professional club but eventually returns to his less affluent amateur friends at S.C. Linda; *Der König der Mittelstürmer* [*The King of the Centre-*

Above: *Die elf Teufel* (1927).
Left: A poster for Max Schmeling's debut film, *Liebe im Ring* (1930).

Forwards] starred Paul Richter as the centre-forward for Alemannia who has to overcome his father's aversion to football and finally leads his team to victory in a cup final. Mountaineering was also regarded as a sport, and films on the subject included *The Holy Mountain* (p. 180), *The White Hell of Pitz Palu* (p. 228), and *Storm over Mont Blanc* (see below). *White Ecstasy* (1930) was a comedy about winter sports, with Leni Riefenstahl as a skiing beauty. Gymnastics was dominant among the sports featured in *Ways to Strength and Beauty* (p. 152), while working-class sport featured in *Whither Germany?* (p. 270).

Society

While change was not apparent in equal measure at all levels of society – owing to shortages of jobs, money, living space, electricity and other basic needs – there was visible progress in some areas, especially in cities. In 1919, German women obtained the right to vote and to run for office, but they remained underrepresented in political parties as well as in official posts. On the other hand, the number of working women rose, and there was more investment in education for girls. Changes in moral attitudes and increasing self-confidence gave rise to the 'New Woman', who could display her emancipation in fields such as advertising, fashion and sport. Initially, these 'New Women' came from the upper middle classes, but after the mid-1920s this soon became a mass cultural movement. A lot of the ideas stemmed from the US, and bobbed hair, cigarettes and knee-length dresses all became fashionable.

Female office workers became a target group for magazines such as *Frauenwelt*, *Die Dame* and *Elegante Welt*. Coffee circles were a popular leisure activity, and in 1923, the celebration of *Muttertag* or Mother's Day was introduced. More importantly, however, women were expected to develop a will of their own, which of course was manifested in the way they expressed themselves. In their leisure time, this meant activities such as dancing, the cinema and sport.

Posters for *Berlin: Symphony of a Great City* (1927), *Ways to Strength and Beauty* (1925) and *People on Sunday* (1930).

Wilhelm Prager's Ufa film *Ways to Strength and Beauty* (p. 152) conjures up one side of this era, harking back historically to physical culture in the form of dance and gymnastics. This was a rather idealized film with educational aspirations. Another side of German society is illustrated by Walther Ruttmann's *Berlin: Symphony of a Great City* (p. 198), a montage film depicting twenty-four hours in the life of a city. A third side can be seen in *People on Sunday* (p. 238), which presents a realistic portrait of contemporary society in a movie that is silent but nonetheless vividly captures all its real-life characters.

Literature

A large number of German authors flourished during the Weimar Republic. Johannes R. Becher was a self-confessed left-winger who for a long time was a member of the Expressionist circle, and described himself as belonging to the 'federation of proletarian-revolutionary writers'. Gottfried Benn,

Magazines such as *Die Woche* and *Elegante Welt*, and brands such as Leichte Regatta cigarettes aimed to appeal to the modern woman.

doctor, lyric poet and essayist, was opposed to Becher and championed an art that was detached from politics. His literary work was well respected, but his initial proximity to National Socialism resulted in long-term damage to his reputation. Bertolt Brecht was active in many literary fields, but made his name mainly as an ardently left-wing playwright during the late 1920s. His obsessions also made their mark on his dealings with the film industry. Together with Erich Engel he made the Karl Valentin film *Mysteries of a Barbershop,* went to court to stop the filming of *The Threepenny Opera* (p. 248), and played an active role in making the paradigmatic, proletarian *Whither Germany?* Alfred Döblin, a qualified neurologist, was also aligned with the left, wrote prose and essays, and enjoyed great success with his novel *Berlin-Alexanderplatz*; he also co-wrote the screenplay for its first film adaptation in 1931 (p. 260). The bulk of Lion Feuchtwanger's literary work was historical novels, the first of which was *Jew Suess*, filmed in Great Britain in 1934. Leonhard Frank was the socially engaged author of many novels, novellas and plays, some of which were also filmed in the late 1920s. Becher, Brecht, Döblin, Feuchtwanger and Frank all emigrated in 1933.

Gerhart Hauptmann was recognized as a major dramatist, was awarded the Nobel Prize in 1912, and was regarded as a naturalist. Many of his plays were filmed during the Weimar Republic as well as in the Nazi era.

Erich Kästner was much loved, especially for his children's books, of which *Emil and the Detectives*, *Pünktchen and Anton* and *The Flying Classroom* were published during the Weimar years. *Emil and the Detectives* was made into a very successful film by Gerhard Lamprecht in 1931 (p. 266). Kästner was vehemently opposed to the Nazis and survived their regime despite a ban on his work. He continued to write, under a pseudonym.

In the 1920s the brothers Heinrich and Thomas Mann were regarded as major authors, and Thomas was awarded the Nobel Prize in 1929. Heinrich campaigned for an alliance between the Communists and the Social Democrats, but in 1933 both brothers fled into exile.

Else Lasker-Schüler wrote poetry, prose and plays, and her circle of friends included the film director F. W. Murnau. Anna Seghers published her first novella in 1928: *Revolt of the Fishermen of Santa Barbara*. Lasker-Schüler and

All Quiet on the Western Front (1930).

Seghers, who were both Jewish, also found themselves forced to emigrate in 1933.

Kurt Tucholsky was regarded as a great all-rounder in Weimar literary circles: he wrote novels, poems, songs and cabaret sketches, and he was a popular journalist and publicist, as well as co-editor of *Weltbühne*. He was also a globetrotter, and spent most of his life after 1924 abroad, working for a time as Paris correspondent for the *Vossische Zeitung*. The essayist, dramatist and storyteller Arnold Zweig had two major successes with his novels *The Case of Sergeant Grischa* and *Young Woman of 1914*. He too had to emigrate in 1933.

It is striking how many of the greatest Weimar authors were of Jewish extraction. Just like the left-wingers, they were driven out of Germany, leaving behind a cultural gap that could never be filled.

It is also necessary to consider Austrian authors, who wrote in German although they did not necessarily wish to be considered German. They included Hermann Broch, Hugo von Hofmannsthal, Karl Kraus, Robert Musil, Alfred Polgar and Stefan Zweig. During the 1920s, their work was extremely well known in Germany.

However, the literary world suffered from a lack of widespread popularity. With just a few exceptions, books were printed in very limited runs, and were known only among intellectual or specialist circles. During the 'Roaring Twenties', the spotlight tended to shine on the stars of stage and screen, and authors continually complained that they were left in the shadows. Occasionally some would find themselves exposed to the bright lights for a short time. One of these luminaries was Erich Maria Remarque, who in 1928 wrote *Im Westen nichts Neues*, which was serialized in the *Vossische Zeitung*. The novel was filmed in the US as *All Quiet on the Western Front* (1930) and made its author a household name all over the world. In Germany, however, the film became a controversial victim of censorship. Vicki Baum was born in Vienna, worked for the Berlin publisher Ullstein from 1926 to 1931, and became internationally famous for her novel *Menschen im Hotel* (1929), which was filmed in the US in 1932 as *Grand Hotel*, clearing the way for her to go to California. Irmgard Keun made her reputation with two novels: *Gilgi – One of Us* (1931) and *The Artificial Silk Girl* (1932), in which a key theme is dreams of the cinema. The first of these novels was filmed under the title *One of Us* in 1932, starring Brigitte Helm and Gustav Diessl.

Other popular authors during this period were Karl May and Hedwig Courths-Mahler. Aesthetic norms in literature were divided into two relatively rigid categories: art for the intellectuals and the middle classes, and popularist trivia for the rest of the population.

Democracy had been abolished and the Nazis were in full control when, on 10 May 1933, books were burned in German university towns to symbolize the outlawing of all Jewish, Marxist and pacifist authors. The writers named in this ritual burning included Heinrich Mann, Ernst Glaeser, Erich Kästner, Sigmund Freud, Theodor Wolff, Erich Maria Remarque, Alfred Kerr, Kurt

Tucholsky and Carl von Ossietzky. These events were captured by chilling film footage and sound recordings.

Writers and Film

During the Weimar Republic, the relationship between literature and film was always ambivalent. Authors watched the rise of the new medium with some degree of envy; they were pleased to have their work filmed (Thomas Mann, Hauptmann, Hofmannsthal, Remarque, Döblin, Schnitzler), but were rarely invited to write screenplays themselves. Some also had their doubts about the medium itself, as expressed back in 1914 by Kurt Pinthus's *Kinobuch*. Many of them expressed in no uncertain terms the view that their literary art was of higher aesthetic value, and that film was merely an industrial product for the masses. Alfred Döblin's comment from 1922 was typical: 'The writer's instrument is language. Film does not speak. What does the writer have to do with film? The author – when needed – has imagination. Film shatters it, cripples it, dwarfs it, perverts it, by forcing it onto a single level – the visual.' Thomas Mann agreed: 'I believe – forgive me – that film has little to do with art, and I consider it misguided to apply to film criteria taken from the realm of art' (1928).

The trivialization of film was blamed on the US, which had imposed its stars and its standard genres on the European cinema. The fall of the Empire had also destabilized the idealistic, humanistic system of values embraced by the educated classes in Germany. The gates were now wide open for the entertainment industry. Faced with competition from jazz, cabaret and sport, the literary world found itself in difficulties. However, it was precisely at this time that German cinema began to claim success that was not only economic but also aesthetic. Thanks to the creative talents of Lubitsch, Lang, Murnau, Mayer, Freund and more, it was able to break free from the restrictions of literature and demonstrate its artistic autonomy.

Theatre

In 1920, the theatre was roughly 3,000 years old, and the cinema a mere twenty-five. On one hand, there were and are fundamental differences between theatre (live and tangible) and cinema (reproducible but intangible). On the other hand, theatre and film both depend on actors and plots. In the 1910s, cinema tried to emulate theatre in order to escape from its reputation as a form of trivial sideshow entertainment and gain recognition as an art form that was acceptable to the middle classes. The large cinemas – especially those built during the 1920s – were designed along the same architectural lines as the typical theatres. Actors and actresses increasingly began to commute between stage and film studio, and it was only logical that theatre directors too should become interested in film, because in both cases the work involved directing actors; if necessary, they could leave cinematography to the camera team.

Grand Hotel (1932).

Left: *Revolt in the Reformatory* (1930).
Right: *The Captain of Köpenick* (1931).

Nevertheless, the theatre continued to lead its own independent and privileged life. Although there were many private theatres, the majority were municipal or state run, with a ready-made, eager but also critical audience. Issues of the day could be addressed through both contemporary and classical plays. Berlin was the theatrical capital, but major theatres in cities like Dresden, Munich, Mannheim and Hamburg staged plays whose impact went beyond local borders. Until the mid-1920s, the dominant style was Expressionism, with its messages, visions and concept of the 'New Man'.

Major dramatists in this sphere were Ernst Barlach, Bertolt Brecht, Georg Kaiser, Ernst Toller and Friedrich Wolf, while the best-known directors were Jürgen Fehling, Otto Falckenberg and Leopold Jessner. Star actors included Werner Krauss, Fritz Kortner, Heinrich George and Ernst Deutsch, in what was evidently a domain dominated by men. They ruled the theatrical roost with their physical presence and their resonant voices.

By the mid-1920s, however, the atmosphere on stage became quieter and more relaxed; this modern style was called *Neue Sachlichkeit* or New Objectivity, and it came from the fields of art, literature and photography. The focus was no longer on imagination and vision but on the world 'as it is' – i.e. authenticity and realism. The most prominent writers now were Bertolt Brecht, born in Augsburg (*The Threepenny Opera*, *Saint Joan of the Stockyard*, *The Mother*), Marieluise Fleisser, born in Ingolstadt (*Purgatory in Ingolstadt*, *Pioneers in Ingolstadt*), and the Austrian Ödön von Horvath (*The Belle Vue*, *Tales from the Vienna Woods*, *Faith, Hope and Charity*). Their style was laid back, disillusioned, laconic, sometimes cynical, and their sympathies lay with the 'little people', the proletariat.

The range of genres included topical and folk plays. The former usually dealt with very concrete subjects such as abortion (*§ 218* by Carl Credé-Hoerder), rearmament (*Giftgas über Berlin* [*Poison Gas Over Berlin*] by Martin Lampel), the right to strike (*Heer ohne Helden* [*Army Without Heroes*] by Anna Gmeyner), incarceration (*Revolte im Erziehungshaus* [*Revolt in the Reformatory*] by Martin Lampel), or a combination of these themes (*Hoppla, We're Alive* by Ernst Toller). The best-known author of folk plays was Carl Zuckmayer (*The Merry Vineyard*, *Slaughterhouse*, *The Captain of Köpenick*). His works were banned in 1933, and he went into exile.

Competing with middle-class theatre were the revues, as presented in Berlin during the 1920s at venues such as the Grosses Schauspielhaus and the Admiralspalast. These were lavishly costumed shows, spectacularly staged and accompanied by popular songs. During the 1930s, they made their way into talking pictures as film operettas.

The Fine Arts

Although the lost war and the search for a new identity presented fresh challenges to practitioners of all the arts in Germany, the majority initially latched onto the style of the early 1910s, but in a more radicalized form. In painting as in other fields, Expressionism was the dominant force, but many artists tended to view the term critically. Styles then diverged into Dada, Constructivism and, in the mid-1920s, New Objectivity. Outstanding artists of the 1920s included Willi Baumeister, Max Beckmann, Otto Dix, Lyonel Feininger, George Grosz, John Heartfield, Erich Heckel, Wassily Kandinsky, Ernst Ludwig Kirchner, Paul Klee, Oskar Schlemmer and Karl Schmidt-Rottluff.

In the 1920s, there was a particularly wide variety of artistic styles and forms. Some painters felt a common link with others, forged through groups or personal friendships, and were active participants in the aesthetic and political debates of the period. Their work was exhibited all over Europe, but because they were opposed to the populist right wing, in 1933 they were either forced to emigrate or to cease painting. Most of them were dismissed by the Nazis as 'degenerate artists'.

Film and Art

It was the desire for recognition that in the late 1910s drove the film industry into making claims to be an art form. It wanted to be taken seriously, and it sought to align itself with recognized images from the realm of the fine arts. It therefore seemed a good idea to integrate the dominant style of the period – namely Expressionism – into the moving pictures. Put like this, it sounds like a targeted strategy, but many of the directors already had close biographical ties to painting.

The two greatest directors of Weimar cinema, Fritz Lang and F. W. Murnau, had a personal and emotional interest in art. It was the inspiration behind the composition of their images, and these links are clearly visible in their work. The film historian Heide Schönemann has made a long and detailed study of these influences in the films of Fritz Lang, and by comparing film images with paintings has even identified echoes of Julius Diez, Otto Dix, Oskar Schlemmer and Magnus Zeller. *Dr Mabuse, the Gambler* (p. 112), *Die Nibelungen* (p. 132) and *Metropolis* (p. 184) are full of allusions to contemporary art, even if these can only be discerned by someone with prior knowledge.

Friedrich Wilhelm Murnau began by studying art history, was friends with the Blue Rider group, and changed his original surname of Plumpe to the place name of Murnau when he went there with some artist friends. His first film (now lost), *The Boy in Blue*, was about the relationship between a painting by Thomas Gainsborough and a boy who lives all alone in a ruined castle. *Nosferatu* (p. 108), *The Last Laugh* (p. 144) and *Faust* (p. 176) would be unimaginable without the scenes taken from paintings with which Murnau was familiar. His allusions hark back to the Romantic and Biedermeier periods.

From top to bottom:
Max Beckmann, *Self-portrait* (1927).
Wassily Kandinsky, portrait by Jacques Moitoret.
Karl Schmidt-Rottluff, *Self-portrait* (1919).
Erich Heckel, *Self-portrait* (1919).

The Boy in Blue (1919), F. W. Murnau's first film.

Among other directors, artistic connections resulted from production techniques or marketing strategies. After the success of *The Cabinet of Dr Caligari* (p. 76), Robert Wiene worked with the painter César Klein on the film *Genuine* (p. 86). However, audiences were unconvinced by the results and the film was a failure. The director Karl Heinz Martin made a radically stylized film out of the Expressionist play *From Morn to Midnight* (p. 84) by Georg Kaiser, and the film industry evidently found it so irritating that it was never released. In Richard Oswald's *Eerie Tales* (p. 68), Death, the Devil and a prostitute come out of paintings and tell horror stories that contain many painterly elements. There is an even more direct link with painting in the first avant-garde films that were made by Walther Ruttmann, Viking Eggeling and Hans Richter. In the second half of the 1920s, however, the links between film and art became increasingly rare or at least unobtrusive.

Film Posters

The 1920s were a boom time for advertising and posters were an important publicity tool. They are omnipresent in the street scenes of Weimar films. Posters and newspaper advertisements were the most important ways of publicizing films. In the early days, the text was dominant, but later the focus switched to dramatic scenes and portraits of the stars. On the facades and in the foyers of the cinemas, posters were meant to lure the spectator in, and on city streets, the latest releases competed for attention through posters stuck on advertising columns and billboards. Naturally there were large numbers of graphic artists who specialized in the genre and even became famous because of their stylistic originality. They included Josef Fenneker, who for many years worked for the Marmorhaus in Berlin, Theo Matejko, who worked in Vienna, Alfred Herrmann, who was responsible for Ufa's posters and used very effective lettering and distorted perspectives, and Jan Tschichold, who was employed by the Phoebus-Palast in Munich and also experimented with typography. While films were still shot and projected in black and white, and colour was only rarely added afterwards, colour could be used very effectively in posters. The production and distribution companies would decide how big individual names should be. The graphic artists' main problem was meeting deadlines. Generally, they had not even seen the films for which they were designing the posters – their only sources of information were production stills and advertising copy.

Architecture

The architecture of the Weimar Republic was influenced mainly by industrial growth and lack of money. Economic problems during the postwar era initially blocked any experimentation or modernization in the field of domestic architecture, and in the cities the shortage of accommodation was so disastrous that, after inflation, state programmes were initiated that were a real challenge to many forward-looking architects.

Prime examples in Berlin were projects carried out by Bruno Taut (the Horseshoe Development in Britz, the 'Uncle Tom's Cabin' Development in Zehlendorf) and Hans Scharoun (Siemensstadt). In 1927, the Weissenhof estate in Stuttgart became a model of its kind: there, under the direction of Ludwig Mies van der Rohe, many champions of the *Neues Bauen* (New Building) movement were able to construct their ideal homes; they included Le Corbusier, Gropius, Poelzig, Scharoun and Taut. However, many new projects got into financial difficulties after the global economic crash. In the early 1930s, the housing shortage became worse than ever, and the National Socialists were quick to make political capital out of the problem.

Many films in the 1920s reflected real life, and one common subject was people's living conditions. Murnau's *The Last Laugh* (p. 144) depicted life in a Berlin backstreet, contrasted with the outward glitter of a large hotel. Fred Sauer's *The Awakening of Woman* dealt with the tenants of an apartment block, with class differences leading to radical conflicts. Dudow's *Whither Germany?* (p. 270) told the story of an unemployed family who have to leave their home in Berlin and move to a tent city. In Ludwig Berger's *I By Day and You By Night* (p. 272), a greedy landlady rents out a room twice over, although in fact this leads to a happy ending when the daytime and night-time tenants fall in love. Fritz Lang's *Metropolis* presents a grim vision of a city of the future, where the rich live above in the light, while the poor live and work underground. A brilliant short documentary by Slatan Dudow, *How the Berlin Worker Lives*, contrasted proletarian living conditions with those of a villa-owner.

Cinema Architecture

The 1920s saw heavy investment in the construction of large new buildings or the conversion of old ones to accommodate cinemas. These were designed to lure people in and to endow the films with a unique atmosphere. The standard was set in Berlin by the converted Ufa-Palast am Zoo, which opened on 18 September 1919 with the premiere of *Madame Dubarry* (p. 62) before an audience of 1,700. This was followed in 1922 by the Mozartsaal in Berlin's Schöneberg district, which for a while became the city's leading cinema, under the direction of Hanns Brodnitz.

Posters for *Dr Mabuse, the Gambler* (1922), *Die Nibelungen* (1924), *Tragedy of the Street* (1927), *Metropolis* (1927), *Asphalt* (1929) and *The Blue Angel* (1930).

From left to right: The Gloria-Palast, the Titania-Palast, the
Universum and the Babylon were among Berlin's biggest cinemas.

The Lichtburg in Essen was the ultimate in
modern cinemas when it opened in 1928.

After the period of inflation, there was a rapid succession of new
cinemas in Berlin: the Capitol (1925) in the Zoo district, designed by
Hans Poelzig; the Gloria-Palast (1926) in the Romanisches Haus on the
Kurfürstendamm, designed by Ernst Lessing and Max Bremer; the Mercedes-
Palast (1926) in Wedding; the second Mercedes-Palast (1927) in Neukölln; the
Titania-Palast (1928) in Steglitzer Schlossstrasse; the Universum (1928) on the
Kurfürstendamm, designed by Erich Mendelssohn (now the Schaubühne am
Lehniner Platz); the Primus-Palast (1928) in Kreuzburg; the Roxy-Palas' (1929)
in Schöneberg; the Babylon (1929) in what was then the Scheunen district,
designed by Hans Poelzig (now a community cinema that shows special
programmes); and the Lichtburg (1929) in the Gesundbrunnen district. Many
cinema names featured the word *Palast*, 'palace', for these were splendid and
symbolic buildings, designed to give the viewing audience the sense that they
were taking part in a special event.

Other German cities also built new cinemas. In Munich, which was
the second most important film centre after Berlin, the cinematic landscape
initially developed more slowly, because the authorities were more focused
on providing housing and regarded movie-going as a luxury. In 1920 the
Rathaus-Lichtspiele opened as a major showcase for film premieres, and in
1924 the Film-Palast opened its doors in Blumenstrasse. In 1926 no less than
fourteen new cinemas were built, including the Schauburg in Elisabethplatz,
the Gloria-Palast in Stiglmaierplatz, and the Phoebus-Palast in Sonnenstrasse,
which for a brief time was the largest cinema in Germany, with 2,200 seats.
Intrusive advertising was frowned on in Munich, and in particular there was a
strict ban on lighting effects.

In Hamburg, too, it was not until the second half of the 1920s that
the construction of 'picture palaces' really took off. The Lessing-Theater
in the Gänsemarkt staged premieres, and there were also the Passage in
Mönckebergstrasse and the Schauburg at the main railway station – but all of
these had fewer than 1,000 seats. First-run showings were overcrowded. Two
young entrepreneurs, Hermann Urich-Sass and Hugo Streit, paved the way
from 1927 onwards. They began with the Schauburg at the Millerntor, and then
built more Schauburg cinemas in Barmbek, Hammerbrook, Nord, Wandsbek
and Uhlenhorst, with over 5,000 seats in all. Ufa took up the challenge, and in
1929 built the Ufa-Palast in the Gänsemarkt, which with 2,660 seats was the

biggest cinema in Europe. However, 1933 saw the demise of the Schauburg company founded by Urich-Sass, who died at the age of forty-eight, and Streit, who fled from Germany after Kristallnacht in 1938.

Finally, mention must also be made of the Lichtburg in Essen. Opened in 1928, it had 2,000 folding seats, an electronic booking system at the box office, and the largest Wurlitzer cinema organ in Europe; it survived decades of expropriation, destruction and reconstruction, mirroring the fate of Germany itself, and is still showing films today. It is now classified as an historical monument and is under a preservation order.

Film Architecture

The architecture of film during the Weimar Republic had only a limited connection with the real-world architecture of the time. It was mainly a creative framework to serve the imagination of the director. Most films were shot in the studio or on sets that had to be purpose built – interiors, facades, houses, palaces, staircases, apartments. They were all the equivalent of stage sets. The set designers of the 1920s were busy people, and they played a major role in establishing the reputation of German cinema.

In the earlier films of Lubitsch and Joe May – *Madame Dubarry*, *Sumarun*, *Veritas vincit* and *The Mistress of the World* – monumental exoticism and regal splendour were the order of the day. Kurt Richter was Lubitsch's set designer, and Paul Leni, Otto Hunte, Erich Kettelhut and Karl Vollbrecht all worked for May. The sets were constructed on studio land in and around Berlin.

Veritas vincit (1919).

In 1920, *Caligari* introduced the Expressionist effects that made Hermann Warm, Walter Röhrig and Walter Reimann world famous. They used distortion and abstraction, and blended painting with film. By contrast, a much more sculptural effect was created by the medieval Prague ghetto designed by the architect Hans Poelzig for *The Golem*. Murnau's *Nosferatu* conveyed a unique atmosphere by mixing location scenes filmed in Wismar, Lübeck and the Carpathians with dark studio sets designed by Albin Grau.

The Golem (1920).

During the 1920s there were six production designers who were held in especially high esteem, mainly through their collaboration with Fritz Lang and F. W. Murnau. They also worked together in varying combinations: Robert Herlth, Otto Hunte, Erich Kettelhut, Walter Röhrig, Karl Vollbrecht and Hermann Warm. All of them were able to continue their work under (and after) the Nazis.

It was the interplay between architecture, space, light and camera that created the characteristic look of German films at this time. The directors had full confidence in their production designers, who between them were always able to come up with solutions, albeit often at a substantial cost.

Film Music

In the mid-1920s, music underwent a liberation that had far-reaching consequences. Technical improvements, the increasing popularity of the

Die Nibelungen (1924).

From left to right:
Giuseppe Becce,
Werner Richard Heymann,
Friedrich Hollaender
and Edmund Meisel.

gramophone record, and the rapid expansion of the radio all meant that music was no longer confined to concert halls and opera houses. Now it could be heard everywhere – in a process of true democratization – from the poorest city apartment blocks to the richest country houses. Classical and modern, jazz and popular songs were available to virtually everyone, although traditionalists complained that this brought the threat of a dumbing-down in musical taste.

Right from the earliest days, music was used as an accompaniment to moving pictures. Fairs and variety shows had already shown how the emotional effects could be amplified by music, and when films became longer and cinemas more middle-class, musical accompaniments accordingly grew more ambitious. Smaller cinemas made do with a single pianist or violinist close to the screen, but the larger picture palaces would have an orchestra pit that held between fifteen and fifty musicians. Under the baton of their conductor, they provided a new musical dimension to enhance the action on the screen.

Cinema organs and other new pieces of equipment were also introduced successfully, but the purpose was always the same: to match the music with the mood and action of the film. Original compositions, however, were the exception – generally, depending on the genre, short compositions were strung together to underline the atmosphere of the scene or to strengthen its emotional impact. There was even an independent market for what were known as 'cue sheets', containing suggestions for music to accompany standard scenes such as partings, quarrels, declarations of love, and deaths.

In Germany, one well-known specialist in film music was the Italian-born composer Giuseppe Becce. As well as his own anthology series of film music called *Kinothek*, he also published the *Handbuch der Film-Musik* (two volumes) in 1927, in collaboration with Hans Erdmann and Ludwig Brav. Becce composed original music for several films, including Murnau's *The Last Laugh* and *Tartuffe*, Pabst's *Secrets of a Soul* and Leni Riefenstahl's *The Blue Light*. He also granted himself licence to quote from the work of other composers.

As the large theatres had small orchestras too, many composers and conductors divided their time between theatre and cinema. Among the best known of these were Paul Dessau, Hanns Eisler, Werner Richard Heymann, Friedrich Hollaender, Edmund Meisel, Robert Stolz and Wolfgang Zeller. Two famous composers, Arnold Schönberg (*Accompaniment to a Film Scene*) and Paul Hindemith (compositions for experimental films by Oskar Fischinger and Hans Richter), took a lively interest in film, but it had no lasting influence on their music.

In the transition from silent to sound movies, music played a central role. *The Jazz Singer* (1927) – the story of a poor Jewish singer who rises to become a Broadway star – was the first successful US talkie. In Germany the honour was shared between Walther Ruttmann's montage film *Melody of the World* (premiered on 12 March 1929) and Hanns Schwarz's feature film *Melody of the Heart* (premiered on 16 December 1929). The melodies in the titles celebrated the launch of film into a new era.

Radios and Gramophones

There were vital developments in the field of acoustics during the 1920s, and these turned radio and the gramophone into mass media. Many inventions and technical improvements were necessary before playing with detector and earphones – initially just a pastime for technically minded amateurs – became an experience available to the whole family. Receivers and horn speakers now made their way into many households. The official date of birth for German radio is regarded as 29 October 1923, when Vox-Haus in Berlin broadcast the first hour of live entertainment. By the beginning of 1925, over half a million people were listening in, and by 1928 the number had reached two million. Listeners had to register and pay a fee, which at the time was 24 marks a year. The first live broadcast of an international football match (Germany vs the Netherlands) took place in April 1926, and on 3 September in the same year, the Berlin radio tower was officially opened. During the first few years, there were no round-the-clock broadcasts – afternoon and evening were prime radio time. Entertainment dominated the broadcasts, with dance music and operettas, but news, sport, reports, lectures and plays also featured. Alongside film, radio rapidly became an integral part of the modern world.

The gramophone record also became established during the 1920s. The use of a microphone and speaker instead of the old horn led to an upsurge in the market, and the record player duly replaced the old-style gramophone. There was fierce competition between record companies, and in 1929 no less than thirty million records were sold in Germany. The number dwindled during the 1930s, however, because money was short and by then the radio had become a powerful rival.

In the film *People on Sunday* (p. 238), one of the five main characters is a salesgirl in a record shop. She takes a record player with her on a weekend outing, and a critical moment occurs when one of the records gets broken during a picnic. Damaged goods can provide emotional motivation, especially when music is involved.

Radios from the 1920s, with earphones and a manual (above) or a horn speaker (below).

A record player appears in *People on Sunday* (1929).

From left to right:
Emil and the Detectives (1931), *The Oyster Princess* (1919)
and *Diary of a Lost Girl* (1929).

Telephones and Typewriters

The telephone also played its part in the history of culture and
communications, and again it was the 1920s that saw it come to the fore.
It now enjoyed extensive private use, and public telephone kiosks were
ubiquitous. In 1930 there were more than 60,000 telephones in Germany's
streets, squares and railway stations. Of course their main use was in the
worlds of business and administration, but the inevitable expansion of
telephone networks led to lower tariffs and an increasing number of private
households having their own phone.

Even in the days of the silent film, the telephone was used as a prop –
often to striking dramatic effect – to pass on news, messages and declarations
of love. It was a way of linking different locations in the story, and the
dialogue was shown as intertitles. Its importance grew with the advent of
talkies. Little 'Tuesday' in *Emil and the Detectives* (p. 266) acts as an information
hub, using his parents' telephone: 'Password: Emil!' In Robert Siodmak's
Looking For His Murderer, every available method – including the telephone – is
used in a last-ditch effort to prevent a hitman from killing Heinz Rühmann.

The 1920s also saw increasing mechanization of the writing process,
in so far as the typewriter took a prominent place on the office desk, and
secretaries became an increasingly important part of office life. There
were now template forms that had to be learned for certain types of
correspondence, and 'typist' was a recognized profession.

In silent films, of course, the rattle of the typewriter could not be
heard, but it became a familiar piece of office equipment, almost always
connected with women and their flying fingers. The bosses dictated the
messages. In Lubitsch's *The Oyster Princess* (p. 60), the cigar-smoking American
'Oyster King' Mr Quaker is shown with an entire audience in the room,
following every rhythmic beat of his dictation.

Another popular medium was the postcard, on which short messages,
congratulations or greetings from a holiday resort could be sent. It usually had
an appealing image on one side, and a small space for the text and address on
the other. In the 1920s there was great demand for star postcards, with images
of the famous actors and actresses of the day. These also became collectors'

items, and the space could be used for autographs. The firm of Ross was regarded as market leader in this particular genre.

The Press

The main source of information and the main influence on public opinion during the 1920s was the newspaper. Democracy benefited from the wide variety of daily papers that provided the country with news, views and current affairs every morning and indeed at other times of the day. The economic basis of many newspapers was generally regarded as unstable, and behind them were the proprietors, some large and some small (the Conservative Alfred Hugenberg, August Scherl, the Ullsteins, the Communist Willi Münzenberg), who had no compunction about making a profit out of an emergency.

Newspapers that were widely read included the *8-Uhr Abendblatt*, the *Berliner Volkszeitung*, the *B.Z. am Mittag*, the *Berliner Lokal-Anzeiger*, the *Deutsche Allgemeine Zeitung*, the *Montag Morgen* or MM, the *Neue Berliner Zeitung* (later *12-Uhr-Blatt*), *Tempo*, the *Neue Zeit* and *Die Welt am Abend*. In 1929, Berlin had 147 daily and weekly newspapers.

There were three newspapers above all that set the tone. The *Berliner Börsen-Courier* was originally devoted purely to financial matters, but later it also devoted sections to politics, sport and culture. On the political spectrum, it was regarded as left-wing liberal. It was published twice daily, and in the 1920s its circulation was around 40,000. On the cultural side, Oskar Loerke as literary critic, Oskar Bie as art critic, and Herbert Ihering as theatre and film critic all had strong reputations.

The *Berliner Tageblatt* was generally regarded as the most influential newspaper in the Weimar Republic. It was also published twice a day, and had a circulation of around 250,000. Its editor-in-chief was the writer Theodor Wolff. From 1919 until 1933, Alfred Kerr was in charge of the theatre section, and he wrote film reviews as well. Freelance contributors included Erich Kästner, Alfred Polgar and Kurt Tucholsky.

The chief editor of the *Vossische Zeitung* steered a liberal course, which in the mid-1920s gave it a circulation of about 60,000. Monty Jacobs was in charge of the feature pages, and one of the film critics was Heinz Pol.

The political parties also had their own newspapers. *Vorwärts* was the main organ of the Social Democrats, *Die Rote Fahne* belonged to the KPD (Communist Party), and the National Socialists had the *Volkische Beobachter*. All of these kept a close eye on the world of film.

The *Frankfurter Zeitung* (founded in 1856) was a liberal newspaper famous for its feature articles. Among those who worked on it were Bernard von Brentano, Bernhard Dibold, Heinrich Hauser and Joseph Roth. From 1922, Siegfried Kracauer also wrote for the feature section; he went to Berlin in 1930 to report from there, and emigrated in 1933.

In Munich, the *Münchner Neuesten Nachrichten* was the newspaper with the strongest traditions, while in Hamburg the *Hamburger Anzeiger*

The *Berliner Tageblatt*.

The *Vossische Zeitung*.

Die literarische Welt and *Der Querschnitt*.

Two left-wing publications: *Die Links-Kurve* and the *Arbeiter-Illustrierte Zeitung*.

From left to right: Kurt Pinthus, Herbert Ihering and Siegfried Kracauer.

was the most widely read, and in Cologne it was the *Kölnische Zeitung*.

Magazines

Magazines and periodicals also enjoyed a boom during the 1920s, but the target groups for these were extremely varied. On the one side were the intellectuals, who expected a high standard of cultural discourse and were catered for by magazines such as *Die Weltbühne* and *Das Tagebuch*, the *Deutsche Rundschau*, *Der Querschnitt* and *Die literarische Welt*. On the other, a far bigger reading public wanted entertainment and news from the wider world. They enjoyed the *Berliner Illustrirte Zeitung* and *Die Woche*, the *Elegante Welt* and *Die Dame*. In the mid-1920s the market expanded considerably. New magazines included *Das Leben*, *Uhu* and *Das Magazin*, as well as the *Arbeiter-Illustrierte Zeitung*. *Die Gartenlaube* remained popular, and anyone who wanted to see the funny side of life could read the satirical magazine *Simplicissimus*.

Film Criticism

During the 1920s, German film criticism had already reached a relatively high standard, but it had major problems with its own image. One difficulty was the fact that critics had very few column inches at their disposal. The daily papers were thinner than they are today, and feature articles were confined to the lower sections of the interior pages. These were referred to as *unterm Strich* – literally 'below the line', but also with a figurative meaning of 'not up to scratch'. It was customary to review several films together, which meant only a few lines for each one, and there was controversy over whether these should be devoted to description, aesthetics or ideology.

Kurt Pinthus, author of the *Kinobuch* (1913), wrote for the *8-Uhr-Abend* and *Das Tagebuch*, and from the mid-1920s onwards also worked in radio. Willy Haas, editor of the *Film-Kurier*, publisher of the *Literarische Welt* and himself a scriptwriter (*Joyless Street*), was an experimentalist who had a great affinity with the cinema; he wrote with what he called 'active proximity' to the film, and felt himself to be a 'co-producer'. Hans Siemsen, who worked on the *Weltbühne* and edited the *8-Uhr-Abend*, was regarded as an aggressive critic who enjoyed having his say in public discussions. He quarrelled with Willy Haas, helped to make Charlie Chaplin famous in Germany, and fought to end discrimination against homosexuality. Heinz Pol wrote initially for the *Vossische Zeitung*, but then for political reasons switched to the Communist *Welt am Abend*. His criteria were ideological, and he also wrote novels dealing with contemporary issues. Herbert Ihering, theatre and film critic for the *Berliner Börsen-Courier*, had a discerning eye for cinematic quality, and focused heavily on the actors. Siegfried Kracauer, who wrote for the *Frankfurter Zeitung*, was unquestionably the leading film critic of the day, and as a sociologist and

essayist also observed and reported on everyday life in the big city. His essay
'Die kleinen Ladenmädchen gehen ins Kino' ['The Little Shopgirls Go to the
Cinema'] was an analysis of contemporary film. His credo was: 'The film critic
of quality is only imaginable as a social critic.' Other critics of quality in the
late 1920s were Bernard von Brentano (*Frankfurter Zeitung*), Axel Eggebrecht
(*Weltbühne*), Hanns G. Lustig (*Tempo*), and Hans Sahl (*Montag-Morgen*). It is
also worth noting that Alfred Kerr, Alfred Polgar and Kurt Tucholsky wrote
film reviews as well.

Covers of *Kinematograph* and *Lichtbild-Bühne*.

Film Magazines

There were several specialist film magazines during the time of the Weimar
Republic. The *Kinematograph*, a weekly 'organ for the entire art of projection',
was founded in 1907 and offered a great deal of information but very little
in the way of serious criticism; the *Lichtbild-Bühne*, founded in 1908, was the
'specialist organ for the sphere of cinematographical theatre practice', with
information aimed especially at cinema owners; the same group was also
targeted by the *Reichsfilmblatt*, the 'organ for the Reich Association of German
cinema owners', which first appeared in 1922; *Kinotechnik*, founded in 1919,
was a magazine for technicians; and last but by no means least the *Film-Kurier*,
also founded in 1919, was a 'daily newspaper for film, variety, art, fashion,
sport, and the stock market', which at its peak had a circulation of 10,000 and
provided a bridge between the specialist press and the general public. Its main
focus was naturally on film, and it provided information about personalities,
productions and premieres, contained advertisements and supplements,
and published interviews and reviews. Its first editor-in-chief was Willy
Haas, followed by Ernst Jäger, and among its leading critics were Hans Feld
and Lotte H. Eisner. In March 1933, it began to decline to the levels of the
conformist press, and in due course the Jewish publisher Alfred Wiener and
many of his old colleagues went into exile.

Front page of the *Film-Kurier*.

Catering for the general public was a parallel publication, *Illustrierter
Film-Kurier*, which was a running programme for individual films and became
a collector's item. Up to March 1933, it ran for 1,900 issues altogether.

There were also popular magazines for filmgoers: *Bunte Filmblätter*, *Film
im Bild*, *Film-Brettl*, *Der Filmfreund*, *Die Film-Tribüne*, *Die Filmwoche*, *Illustrierte*

Covers of the *Illustrierter Film-Kurier*, advertising the
films *Joyless Street* (1925), *Asphalt* (1929), *Mother Krause's
Journey to Happiness* (1929), *Berlin-Alexanderplatz* (1931)
and *The Blue Angel* (1930).

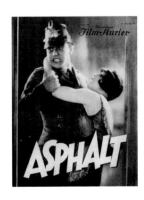

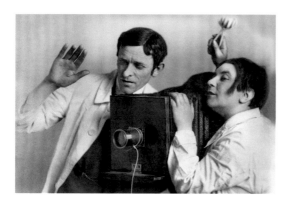

A scene from *Im Photoatelier* (1932).

camera, he was able to move fast and to take his photographs without using a flash. His book *Berühmte Zeitgenossen in unbewachten Augenblicken* [*Famous Contemporaries in Unguarded Moments*] was published in 1931. He died in Auschwitz in 1944.

Like Salomon, Alfred Eisenstaedt regarded himself as a photojournalist, and from 1927 he worked for the *Berliner Tageblatt*, photographing actors and actresses and writers; he also reported on the award of the Nobel Prize to Thomas Mann, but emigrated to New York in 1935. It was he who took the only known photograph of Marlene Dietrich and Leni Riefenstahl together (p. 37).

There is a lovely homage to photography in the film *People on Sunday*. A sequence on the lakeside beach at Wannsee, Berlin, shows a photographer at work, and a montage of the results is slotted in as a series of stills. In the short film *Im Photoatelier* [*In the Photographer's Studio*], Karl Valentin and Liesl Karlstadt as assistant and apprentice cause chaos in the studio while their boss is away. Handling a camera can be a funny business.

Film Photography

The relationship between film and photography was always very close. Films need photographs to represent them. Their beauty and imagination, art and popularity are all unthinkable without the pictures reproduced in newspapers and magazines, books and periodicals, display cases and cinemas themselves. Still shots of scenes, postcards of stars, posters – all these visual references are essential for the film to make its presence felt outside the cinema. This is why stills photographers are present during film shoots, because only then can they capture the highlights of the story and, above all, the impact of the characters. They freeze the motion of a moving picture, but generally their work only begins when a scene is finished. Then the actors repeat selected moments, and pose for the camera.

German stills from the 1920s are often dark in tone, in contrast to American stills of that time. There, the emphasis was more on entertainment, and so the sun was usually shining, whereas in Germany it was the twilight and the shadows that predominated. Generally the streets in these photographs are badly lit. The atmosphere of the interiors stems mainly from the layout of doors, tables, curtains, and from the choreography of the actors, their positioning and their gestures.

Most stills photographers remained anonymous, because they had been hired by the production company but were rarely employed fulltime. Exceptions were the Binder Studio, Horst von Harbou, Hans Natge and Frieda Riess. This book owes its existence to the art of stills photography.

Working Photographs

For historical purposes, working photographs of film sets are particularly revealing because they allow us to look behind the scenes, however briefly. Evidently it was traditional in those days to take a large group shot of the

whole team smiling happily as they
looked at the photographer. Some
of the sets are extremely impressive,
e.g. for the film *I.N.R.I.* at the
Spandau Studio, and for *Metropolis* in
Babelsberg. The main focus of working
photographs was, of course, the film
camera, behind which the director,
cameraman and assistants would all be
hard at work. But shots that show the
director doubling as a make-up artist
can be an added attraction.

Film Production

Ufa (Universum-Film AG) was founded
in 1917, to bring a new dimension to

From left to right and
top to bottom, set
photographs from:
I.N.R.I. (1923),
Emil and the Detectives (1931),
Metropolis (1927),
Schinderhannes (1927),
The Wonderful Lies of Nina Petrovna (1929),
Metropolis (1927),
Metropolis (1927).

the war at home and on the front. The Deutsche Bank and the Deutsches
Reich invested a good 25 million marks as this was deemed to be in the
national interest. It had no effect on the outcome of the war, but in the new
republic, Ufa immediately occupied a key position, as it united under one roof
three separate strands of the film industry: it had at its disposal the largest
production capacity (stars, directors and studios), had a huge distribution
network, and owned the largest chain of cinemas in Germany.

Of course there were many rival production companies that made
substantial contributions to the quantity and variety of German films.
Some were small, and were founded by directors (Richard Eichberg, Rudolf
Meinert, Richard Oswald, Lupu Pick), but there were also larger, well-known
companies such as Decla Film in Berlin (founded in 1915 by Erich Pommer)
and Deutsche Bioscop, the two of which merged in 1920 to become Decla-
Bioscop, which in turn was taken over by Ufa in 1923. In Munich, several film
companies came together in 1919 to form Münchner Lichtspielkunst AG,
known as 'Emelka', which was situated in Geiselgasteig and developed into a
major corporation but did not survive the switch to talkies. It was succeeded
in 1932 by Bavaria Film AG.

The transition from war to peace was almost seamless as far as the film industry was concerned. People yearned for distraction and entertainment, which they found in comedies and especially the detective serials that were very popular at the time. The heroes of these were exclusively Anglo-Saxon, with names such as Stuart Webbs, Joe Deebs, Tom Shark and Miss Clever. These exciting tales were told at speed, and the focus was less on the logical explanation of a crime than on the dangers the heroes found themselves in. One of the best-known stars of these adventures was Harry Piel, who never used a stunt double.

The lifting of censorship cleared the path for so-called *Aufklärungsfilme*, or 'educational films', which combined frank portrayals of sex with information on 'social hygiene'. As depictions of the formerly unfilmable, they aroused a great deal of attention.

The Year 1919

The first year of peace was a great one for Ernst Lubitsch. During the war he had become extremely popular, first as an actor and then also as a director, a master of comedy and also of melodrama (*Carmen*, 1918). In this one year, he made six films that covered the whole range of his genius. He began with the comedy *Meyer aus Berlin*, which he directed while also taking the leading role. This was followed immediately by *My Wife, the Movie Star*, an insider comedy starring the cinema goddess Ossi Oswalda. Then came *The Oyster Princess* (p. 60) a satirical fairy tale about the culture clash between Europe and America. Next Lubitsch filmed the Strindberg play *Intoxication* with Asta Nielsen (unfortunately the film is now lost), but he reached a peak with the costume film *Madame Dubarry* (p. 62), a lush historical drama set at the time of the French Revolution. The film became a worldwide success. Then for Christmas, Lubitsch released *The Doll* (p. 70), another comedy starring Ossi Oswalda. Incredibly, the director was still only twenty-seven years old.

The careers of Fritz Lang and F. W. Murnau also began in 1919, but they were then very much in the shadow of directors such as Joe May and Richard Oswald. May came from Austria, and in 1914 he founded his own production company in Berlin, initially making successful detective series, but then to greet the new republic he made his first spectaculars: *Veritas vincit* (p. 58), a three-and-a-half-hour epic starring his wife Mia May, followed by the mammoth production *Mistress of the World* (p. 72), an adventurous journey through China, Africa, America and Europe.

Richard Oswald, also an Austrian, was at home in many genres, was regarded as the originator of the *Aufklärungsfilm*, and also discovered Anita Berber and Conrad Veidt. In 1919 he released three films: *Prostitution* (a plea for legalization), *Different from the Others* (an appeal for the acceptance of homosexuality) and *Eerie Tales* (a horror fantasy; see p. 68). Oswald took risks and suffered a few failures, but remained a major figure in Weimar cinema until 1933.

Directors Ernst Lubitsch and Joe May (1919).

In the summer of 1919, Robert Wiene directed a film that became
an international legend: *The Cabinet of Dr Caligari* (p. 76), the first totally
Expressionist film. The subject matter came from the horror genre, but the
full effect was created by the stylized sets, lighting, make-up, intertitles and
the body language of the actors. The lead roles were played by Werner Krauss,
Conrad Veidt and Lil Dagover.

Poster for *The Cabinet of Dr Caligari* (1920).

Expressionist Film

The aesthetic approach that influenced *The Cabinet of Dr Caligari* came from
art and theatre. The Expressionist artists who flourished after the turn
of the century set out to give subjective expression to their thoughts and
feelings, without regard for artistic tradition. The film took over every formal
element it could use in its own medium: painted sets, slanting shadows,
passionate intertitles, alienating make-up, stylized acting seemingly without
psychological motivation. The themes were derived from Romanticism:
schizophrenic human nature, the fascination of demonic beings, and in the
delusions with which the main characters were afflicted, tyrants appeared
who with hindsight were identified as premonitions of Hitler. An outstanding
analysis on this subject, a 'psychological history of German films' written by
Siegfried Kracauer, was entitled *From Caligari to Hitler*.

However, it would be wrong to overestimate the part played by
Expressionist films in the Weimar cinema. Basically, apart from *Caligari*,
only eight films between 1920 and 1925 can truly be called Expressionist.
From Morn to Midnight (p. 84) by Karl Heinz Martin is the story – told with
many lighting effects – of a bank clerk, expressively played by Ernst Deutsch,
who breaks out of his daily routine, only to end up committing suicide.
The film was not widely shown. Robert Wiene's *Genuine* (p. 86) is about a
vampiric woman (played by Fern Andra), with sets and costumes by the artist
César Klein. *The Golem* (p. 88) by Carl Boese and Paul Wegener contained
architectural visions by Hans Poelzig. Karl Heinz Martin's *Das Haus zum Mond*
(*The House on the Moon*) is about a waxwork maker who falls in love with a
sleepwalker as well as with a wax model of her, and eventually loses his mind.

Robert Wiene's *Raskolnikov* is an adaptation of Dostoevsky's *Crime
and Punishment*, and was made with Russian actors; the sets and lighting
effects feature clear allusions to Expressionism. *Warning Shadows* (p. 122) by
Arthur Robison is a drama about insane jealousy cured by a shadow puppet
show; Albin Grau's buildings and costumes are Expressionist in style. Paul
Leni's *Waxworks* (p. 142) is divided into three episodes, depicting Harun al-
Rashid, Ivan the Terrible and Jack the Ripper behaving as horrifically as you
might expect, but in the end it turns out these were simply the nightmares
of a poet; the film is full of Expressionist moments, especially in the Jack
the Ripper section. The same applies to Murnau's *Nosferatu* (p. 108), with
its sets and costumes by Albin Grau, and in Lang's *Die Nibelungen* (p. 132),
Walther Ruttmann's 'Dream of the Falcon' sequence is also Expressionist.

The Spiders (1919).

Even Lubitsch's *The Wildcat* (p. 98) contains some elements of the Expressionist style.

The Magnificent Seven: Part 1

The fact that the period between 1919 and 1925 constitutes what is artistically the most interesting phase of German cinema is due to seven creative talents who at the time were major international figures, but who for various reasons left Germany or were banned from working. They were the directors Ernst Lubitsch, Fritz Lang and F. W. Murnau, the writer Carl Mayer, the cinematographer Karl Freund, the producer Erich Pommer, and – representing set design in general – the architect Hans Poelzig.

Lubitsch was born in Berlin, and made his international breakthrough with *Madame Dubarry* (p. 62). Before he went to Hollywood in 1922, he directed three other costume dramas in German (*Anne Boleyn, Sumurun* and *The Loves of Pharaoh*), three successful comedies, and a chamber drama called *The Flame*, starring Asta Nielsen. His mastery of different genres qualified him to be called an all-rounder, and his early departure to Hollywood was a bitter blow for German cinema, although it did earn the Americans' respect for German professionalism.

Fritz Lang was born in Vienna, studied painting and architecture, became a screenwriter, moved to Berlin in 1918, and by 1919 was directing four films (*The Half-Caste, Master of Love, The Spiders* and *Harakiri*). His big breakthrough came in 1921, with a German 'folk tale', *Destiny* (p. 102). Three major films followed, which Lang made with his wife, the writer Thea von Harbou, and the producer Erich Pommer: the two-part thriller *Dr Mabuse, the Gambler* (p. 112), the two-part epic *Die Nibelungen* (p. 132) and the monumental futuristic vision *Metropolis* (p. 184). Although influenced by Expressionism, Lang developed his own individual style, using painterly sets and sophisticated film techniques, and this allowed him to incorporate current political and social themes into his films. With *Metropolis* he stretched Ufa's resources to their utmost capacity. Instead of the 2 million marks that were budgeted for, he spent 5 million marks. The film had to be shortened in order not to overtax the audience, the studio dismissed Pommer, the producer, and Lang himself was put on a tight leash.

Friedrich Wilhelm Murnau's real surname was Plumpe. He was an art historian, began his career as an actor, and between 1919 and 1921 directed nine films with varying subjects, most of which are believed to have been lost. Between 1922 and 1926, apart from a few minor works, Murnau created four films that are regarded as the pinnacle of German silent film: *Nosferatu* (p. 108), a 'symphony in grey' based on Bram Stoker's *Dracula*; *The Last Laugh* (p. 144), a tragicomedy about an ageing hotel porter; *Tartuffe* (p. 166), an idiosyncratic adaptation of Molière's play, starring Werner Krauss; and *Faust* (p. 176), a version of Goethe's famous play. Murnau too was influenced by Expressionism, but his style was given an unmistakable individuality by the visual atmosphere, the mobility of the camera and the fluid editing. Murnau went to Hollywood in 1926, and died in 1931 following a traffic accident in Santa Monica.

Carl Mayer, an Austrian painter, actor and author, was one of the most important influences on the German silent film, even though he never did any directing. His screenplay for *Caligari* made him famous, and he wrote seven more for Murnau, including *The Last Laugh* and *Tartuffe*, as well as working with Lupu Pick (*Shattered*, *New Year's Eve*), Leopold Jessner (*Backstairs*, *Erdgeist*), Arthur von Gerlach (*Vanina*), and it was he who gave Walther Ruttmann the idea for *Berlin: Symphony of a Great City* (p. 198). The precision of his scripts and the sensitive manner in which he collaborated with different directors were his main strengths. Murnau's departure to America marked the end of Mayer's golden age; he quarrelled with Ufa, and emigrated to the UK in 1932.

Karl Freund began his career as a projectionist, but in 1913 became a cameraman, and his self-confidence and extraordinary technical creativity had a huge influence on filmic expression during the 1920s. He worked closely together with Murnau on nine films, including *The Last Laugh* (p. 144), made *The Golem* (p. 88) with Paul Wegener, also worked with Carl Theodor Dreyer on *Michael* (p. 140), E. A. Dupont on *Variety* (p. 162), Fritz Lang on *Metropolis* (p. 184), and was chief cameraman and inspiration behind the concept of Ruttmann's *Berlin: Symphony of a Great City*. He had an amazing ability to give the camera a life and flexibility of its own. He emigrated to America in 1929.

Erich Pommer was a clever businessman who founded the Decla Film Company in 1915 in Berlin. In 1920 this merged with Deutsche Bioscop, to form the second biggest company after Ufa. Beginning with *Dr Caligari*, Pommer was in charge of numerous major productions in the early 1920s, including those of Lang and Murnau. He produced films by the Danish directors Benjamin Christensen (*His Mysterious Adventure*) and Carl Theodor Dreyer (*Michael*), and lavish projects such as Arthur von Gerlach's *Chronicles of the Grey House* (p. 148), Ludwig Berger's *Der verlorene Schuh* [*The Lost Shoe*], E. A. Dupont's *Variety* (p. 162) and Arthur Robison's *Manon Lescaut*. Pommer had an eye for quality and for value, and he thought on an international scale. With *Metropolis*, however, he miscalculated and left Ufa to go and work with Pola Negri in Hollywood. A year later, Ufa brought him back.

The architect Hans Poelzig built the sets for only three films in the first half of the 1920s – *The Golem*, *Living Buddhas* and *Chronicles of the Grey House* – but these were immensely effective and had a lasting impact. His work epitomized the important role of set designers, and he may be taken as a representative for all of them. His vision of the Prague ghetto during the 16th century made a major contribution to the success of *The Golem*. He worked again with the actor who played the Golem, Paul Wegener, on the film *Living Buddhas*, which conveyed an exotic image of India and Tibet. For Arthur von Gerlach's *Chronicles of the Grey House*, Poelzig designed the castle that provides the setting for this family drama. After this, he concentrated on

The Loves of Pharaoh (1921).

Shattered (1921).

Backstairs (1921).

Two stills from *Pandora's Box* (1929).

his own large-scale building projects, which included the I.G. Farben-Haus in Frankfurt am Main and a number of cinemas, but he never entered a film studio again. He died in 1936.

Of these seven giants of the German film industry in the early 1920s, only two were still making German films by the end of the decade.

The 'Chamber' Film

It might be said that Carl Mayer was the creator of the German *Kammerspielfilm* – a term that was derived from the theatrical 'chamber play'. These were films with small casts in a restricted space, and they were produced as a kind of counter to Expressionism, especially between 1921 and 1925. Although they were also shot on studio sets, their focus was on real life and the hopes and dreams of their characters. It was humanity that lay at the heart of each story, and the characters were dominated by their physical needs, or had lost their identity in the chaos of city life, thus mirroring the insecurity of the German middle classes during the period of inflation. Prominent directors of these *Kammerspielfilme* included Lupu Pick, Leopold Jessner, Arthur Robison and Karl Grune. The best-known titles included *Shattered*, *New Year's Eve* (p. 130), *Backstairs* (p. 106) and *Schlagende Wetter* [*Firedamp*]. Carl Mayer and F. W. Murnau's *The Last Laugh* (p. 144) is also a *Kammerspielfilm* in the manner in which it describes the main character's way of life. It was typical of these films that their leading actors often came from the theatre. Psychological dramas of this kind gave the cast plenty of scope for using theatrical techniques.

New Objectivity

From the mid-1920s onwards, an even greater impact than that of the *Kammerspielfilm* was made by a wave of social realist films bracketed under the name of 'New Objectivity'. As with Expressionism, this movement was indebted to forms and approaches derived from art and literature. Absolute truth to life was the aim. External events were presented as they appeared to the camera. Direct perception of the surface of things was the hallmark of a series of montage films, which organized scenes from human life and geographical locations according to strict formal principles. The most famous example remains *Berlin: Symphony of a Great City* (p. 198), a montage of scenes by Walther Ruttmann, who represented twenty-four hours in Berlin almost musically, splitting it up into rhythmic sequences.

G. W. Pabst is generally regarded as having been the most significant director of the New Objectivity movement. His sharp eye for social situations among the middle classes of the mid- and late 1920s led to a series of impressive films dealing primarily with sexuality and eroticism. *Joyless Street* (p. 156) is set in Vienna, but exemplifies the decline of the middle classes at that time; *Pandora's Box* (p. 214) is an adaptation of Wedekind's stories of Lulu, who is murdered in the end; *Diary of a Lost Girl* (p. 224) divides its drama between a reformatory for wayward girls and a brothel.

One late silent film was seen as a model of its kind: *People on Sunday* (p. 238) is an entertaining study of five young people who spend Saturday in the city and Sunday in the country; a lively and lifelike portrait of its time.

Mountain Movies

Looking up from down below, then looking down from up above, views of the heights and later into the distance, the dangers of climbing, isolation in the snow and ice – all of these contributed to the fascinating challenge of a typical German genre of the 1920s: the *Bergfilm* or 'mountain film'. Its hero was the geologist and skiing instructor Arnold Fanck, whose work was truly pioneering. The titles alone evoked myth and adventure: *The Mountain of Fate*, *The Holy Mountain* (p. 180), *The White Hell of Pitz Palu* (p. 228), *Storm over Mont Blanc*, *SOS Iceberg*. Every climb is an adventure. In a love triangle, the drama may be predictable, but nature and the weather are the very opposite – the dangers lie where you cannot see them. There is seldom a happy ending. Generally, any character weakness is punished by death. The cameramen who filmed these stories were also at risk, and they had the added burden of carrying 30 kg of equipment with them. Filming was a dangerous business, and some of the cameramen – such as Sepp Allgeier and Hans Schneeberger – actually made a name for themselves as mountaineers. It was Arnold Fanck who cast the actors Luis Trenker and Leni Riefenstahl in his *Bergfilme*, and later both of them went on to direct films of the same genre themselves.

The White Hell of Pitz Palü (1929).

SOS Iceberg (1932).

Street Films

The so-called 'street film' also dealt with the subject of danger. From the perspective of a house or an apartment, city streets are seen as unsafe, full of menace and temptation. Most of these films take place in the evening or at night, where life outside is very different from life in the shelter of a living room or bedroom. Karl Grune's *The Street* (p. 126) gave this genre its name: a lower-middle-class man comes under the influence of crooks and prostitutes, is imprisoned on suspicion of murder, but is finally released and returns to his wife. The images play with light and shade, and the characters are caught between fear and hope. G. W. Pabst's *Joyless Street* (p. 156), Bruno Rahn's *Tragedy of the Street* (p. 192) and Joe May's *Asphalt* (p. 218) are all examples of the genre. The narrative pattern closely follows that of the melodrama, because these films are not just about social problems but also about the need for love, and about people's hopes and dreams.

Nonetheless, it was a characteristic of Weimar cinema that genres and forms intermingled, and it was only rarely that a film set out to slot itself into one particular pigeonhole.

Historical Films

Ernst Lubitsch's *Madame Dubarry* (p. 62) set a standard for historical films. The public were particularly engrossed by tales from the world of the monarchs, though it was mostly the fortunes and misfortunes of queens and princesses that formed the subject matter – for instance, *Anne Boleyn* (p. 92), whose failure to produce a son (she only managed a daughter) led to her execution. Germany's own favourite queen, Louise of Prussia, also made it to the screen in *Königin Luise*, filmed in two parts with Mady Christians in the title role. The Bavarians had their *Ludwig der Zweite*, directed and played by Wilhelm Dieterle, and at almost the same time (1929), Napoleon found his way into German cinemas: Karl Grune's *Waterloo* starred the French actor Charles Vanel, and in Lupu Pick's *Napoleon at St Helena*, he was played by the German Werner Krauss. In all these films, the mood was pessimistic. The range of biographical films was very wide, from *Lucrezia Borgia* (p. 116), *Marie Antoinette* and *Lola Montez* to *Christopher Columbus*, *Paganini*, *Friedrich Schiller* and *Martin Luther*. The New Testament also figured, with Gregori Chmara playing the crucified Christ in Robert Wiene's *I.N.R.I*, with Henny Porten and Asta Nielsen suffering together as the Virgin Mary and Mary Magdalene.

One particular German favourite was (and still is) Frederick the Great. Between 1920 and 1932, there were no less than eleven films about him, one in two parts, one in four, and on seven occasions he was played by Otto Gebühr, who seems to have been born to play the role.

The Proletarian Film

From the mid-1920s onwards, the Communist and Social Democrat parties, the unions and other left-wing organizations all founded production companies to make 'proletarian' films, which became a genre of their own. Their heroes were destroyed by a range of social contradictions. The forerunners were Gerhard Lamprecht's films – inspired by Heinrich Zille – *Slums of Berlin* (p. 160) and *Children of No Importance*. One of the finest of these working-class films was *Mother Krause's Journey to Happiness* (p. 236), directed by Phil Jutzi for Prometheus Film, which had close ties to the KPD (Communist Party). The scenes seem remarkably authentic.

Werner Hochbaum's *Brothers* was financed by the Hamburg Dockworkers' Union and the SPD (Social Democrats), and used amateur actors to tell the story of the famous general strike in the port of Hamburg in 1896–97. Hans Tintner's *Cyankali*, written by Friedrich Wolf, was independently financed: a pregnant, unemployed shorthand typist and her fiancé find themselves in dire circumstances leading to a botched abortion. The young woman dies, and the film lays the blame on social conditions.

In *Whither Germany?* (p. 270), produced by Prometheus Film and directed by Slatan Dudow, the subject is mass unemployment and the concomitant changes in social relationships. The screenplay (Bertolt Brecht and Ernst Ottwald) and music (Hanns Eisler) were militant, and the two leading roles were played by Hertha Thiele and Ernst Busch, who were both very well known. The film had to be submitted several times to the censors, because it was highly critical of the justice system, the police and the church;

Mother Krause's Journey to Happiness (1929).

Whither Germany? (1932).

it was passed in April 1932, and then banned in 1933. *Whither Germany?* was the last proletarian film of the Weimar Republic.

Documentaries and the Avant-garde

In those days, the term 'documentary' did not exist. The genre was known as the *Kulturfilm*, and encompassed any film with a non-fiction subject: education, industry, advertising and news. The *Kulturfilm* itself could be divided into at least five sub-genres: the city, animals and nature, exploration (including colonial and ethnographic), religion and biography.

One *Kulturfilm* of the 1920s is included in this book: *Ways to Strength and Beauty* (p. 152) by Wilhelm Prager. Its imagery vividly conveys the delight in physical culture at that time, and even earned the plaudits of Siegfried Kracauer. It should not be misinterpreted as a forerunner of Nazi propaganda.

The genre of the avant-garde film was generally referred to in German as *absolute Film* or *abstrakte Film*, creating a strong link with contemporary art. Its main exponents were Walther Ruttmann, Viking Eggeling, Hans Richter and Oskar Fischinger. They played with geometric forms – initially paintings that were brought to life with animation techniques. Prime exanples were Ruttmann's *Opus I – 4*, Richter's *Rhythmus 23* and *Rhythmus 25*, and Eggeling's *Diagonal-Symphonie*.

Ruttmann drew inspiration from France for his *Berlin: Symphony of a Great City* (p. 198), which is more an avant-garde montage than a documentary. In 1929 he experimented with sound and made the film *Melody of the World*, but this was followed by several failures, and he took a job with Ufa as director of industrial and advertising films. Like Ruttmann, Hans Richter used more real shots in his later films (such as *Ghosts Before Breakfast*), and in 1929 he organized the film section of the 'Film und Foto' exhibition in Stuttgart; he also published a book entitled *Filmgegner von heute – Filmfreunde von morgen* [*Film Foes of Today – Film Friends of Tomorrow*]. Oskar Fischinger was another avant-garde filmmaker, who at the end of the 1920s linked abstract forms with combinations of sounds. His *12 Studies* (1927–32) are typical examples. Fischer was also much in demand as an animator, and worked for Fritz Lang on *Woman in the Moon* (p. 230) and for Ufa. He emigrated to America in 1936.

Another unique genre was the silhouette film, developed by Lotte Reiniger, who was able to turn her passion for silhouettes into a profession. Her most famous work, *The Adventures of Prince Achmed* (p. 174), was the first full-length animated film in the history of the cinema.

Actresses

In the 1920s there were no nationwide popularity polls to provide a league table of stars, but the magazines ran their own polls, and it is clear that during the first phase of the Weimar Republic, six actresses were outstanding: Henny Porten was the undisputed queen, followed by Pola Negri, Ossi Oswalda, Mia May, Asta Nielsen and Lil Dagover. Some of them had risen to fame before the

Photomontage publicity still for *Berlin: Symphony of a Great City* (1927) by the photographer Umbo (Otto Umbehr).

war. Apart from Ossi Oswalda, all of them had an aura of timeless detachment that had somehow not yet entered into the modern age. In the early 1930s, after the introduction of talkies, the top six were very different: Lilian Harvey now led the way, followed by Renate Müller, Dolly Haas, Elisabeth Bergner, Brigitte Helm and Gerda Maurus. The faces as portrayed by the camera looked more modern, and they had clearly learned from the productions of the twenties and the manner in which the film industry had evolved.

Actors
In the evaluation of actors, there was an overall distinction between respect and hero-worship. Werner Krauss was recognized for his versatility, while Harry Liedtke was the adored charmer. The top names in the popularity list during the early days of the Weimar Republic were Liedtke, Emil Jannings, Conrad Veidt, Gustav von Wangenheim, Wilhelm Dieterle and Harry Piel. Liedtke was the heart-throb, Jannings the character actor, Veidt the mystery man, Wangenheim the young lover, Dieterle the aristocrat and Piel the bold adventurer.

After the introduction of talkies, the leading men were Willy Fritsch, Hans Albers, Heinz Rühmann, Rudolf Forster, Gustav Fröhlich and Heinrich George. Fritsch was the charming boy from next door, Albers the daredevil who always took charge, Rühmann another charmer, Fröhlich Mr Nice Guy, Forster the gentleman and George the heavyweight.

The Magnificent Seven: Part 2
The second 'golden age' of German film occurred between 1929 and 1932, and was once again due to the creative talents of seven men: the directors Fritz Lang, Max Ophüls, Georg Wilhelm Pabst and Robert Siodmak, the screenwriter Billie Wilder, the composer Werner Richard Heymann and the producer Erich Pommer.

In 1929, Fritz Lang himself produced the science-fiction film *Woman in the Moon* (p. 230) for Ufa, and it was a financial flop. Ufa parted company with him, and he went to Nero-Film, where in 1930, under the producer Seymour Nebenzahl, he made his most important film, *M* (p. 250), the story of a child murderer. It was Lang's first talkie, which had all the qualities of a great artistic experiment, and it is still regarded as a landmark in German film history. *The Testament of Dr Mabuse*, made in 1932, failed to get past the censors in Berlin and was given its premiere in Budapest. On 30 March, Lang went into exile.

The director G. W. Pabst sprang to prominence with *Joyless Street* (p. 156). As a champion of New Objectivity, he made *The Devious Path* in 1928, with Brigitte Helm, and *Pandora's Box* (p. 214) and *Diary of a Lost Girl* (p. 224) in 1929, with Louise Brooks. Four talkies made in the early 1930s – *Westfront 1918*, *The Threepenny Opera* (p. 248), *Comradeship* and *The Mistress of Atlantis* – cemented his reputation, and he continued his career in France and also, during the 1940s, in Nazi Germany. With hindsight, it may be said that the films he made between 1929 and 1932 were his masterpieces.

The Jewish director Robert Siodmak was born in Dresden, made his debut in 1930 with *People on Sunday* (p. 238), and made seven more films before 1933, including *Farewell*, *Looking For His Murderer*, *Inquest* and *The Burning Secret*. The existential fears of his protagonists sounded a new note in the German cinema. In 1933 Siodmak emigrated, first to Paris and then to the US, where he became a pioneer of *film noir*. His brother, the screenwriter Kurt Siodmak, left Germany in 1933 and made his name in America.

The director Max Ophüls, whose real name was Max Oppenheimer, began his career as an actor in the theatre, also worked on radio, and went to Berlin in 1931. He made the feature films *The Company's in Love, The Bartered Bride, Laughing Heirs* and in 1932 his first masterpiece *Liebelei* (p. 274). This was his artistic breakthrough, but there could be no follow-up in Germany because he fled from Berlin the night after the burning of the Reichstag, and went on a perilous journey through Europe before finally ending up in America in 1941.

The Austrian Billie (later Billy) Wilder went to Berlin in 1926 as a journalist, worked as a ghost writer for several screenwriters, and was part of the team that made the film *People on Sunday*. From 1930 onwards, he worked on the stories or screenplays for eleven films, including Robert Siodmak's *Looking For His Murderer*, Gerhard Lamprecht's *Emil and the Detectives* (p. 266), Paul Martin's *A Blonde's Dream* and Géza von Bolváry's *What Women Dream*. Wilder had a talent for weird and wonderful stories and a laconic wit. In 1933 he emigrated, first to Paris and then via Mexico to Hollywood, where he became one of the great directors of American comedy.

The composer Werner Richard Heymann became general music director at Ufa in 1926, wrote the music for Murnau's *Faust* (p. 176) and Lang's *Spies* (p. 206), and between 1930 and 1933 composed the music for fifteen Ufa talkies that set the standard for the genre of the film operetta. These included: *Love Waltz* (with the song 'Du bist das süsseste Mädel der Welt'), *Three Good Friends* ('Ein Freund, ein guter Freund'), *Bombs on Monte Carlo* ('Das ist die Liebe der Matrosen'), *Congress Dances* ('Das gibt's nur einmal, das kommt nicht wieder'), and *A Blonde's Dream* ('Irgendwo auf der Welt'). The stars who performed his songs included Lilian Harvey, Willy Fritsch, Heinz Rühmann, Hans Albers and the Comedian Harmonists. Heymann, who was Jewish, was the greatest songwriter of the early 1930s. He emigrated to Paris in 1933.

The producer Erich Pommer went to Hollywood in 1927 for a year, but then returned to Berlin, where Ufa welcomed him back. Almost symbolically, his first film was called *Homecoming* (p. 210), and that was followed by *Asphalt* (p. 218) and *The Wonderful Lies of Nina Petrovna* (p. 220). Then in less than four years he produced seventeen major sound films, including *Melody of the Heart, Love Waltz, The Blue Angel* (p. 240), *Darling of the Gods, Three Good Friends, Inquest, Congress Dances* (p. 258), *A Blonde's Dream, I By Day and You By Night* (p. 272), *F.P.1 Doesn't Answer* and *The Empress and I*. The directors who worked

Farewell (1930).

Posters for *I By Day and You By Night*
(1932) and *Five of the Jazzband* (1932).

for him included Hanns Schwarz, Wilhelm Thiele, Josef von Sternberg, Robert Siodmak, Erik Charell, Paul Martin, Ludwig Berger and Friedrich Hollaender. Some of the films were made in several languages and became international successes. Erich Pommer, like many of his colleagues, left Germany in 1933.

Dreams and Reality: 1932

The final year of the Weimar Republic was filled with emergency measures, political conflicts, economic problems and shattered hopes. At the time there were 5,000 cinemas in Germany, and 132 new German films were premiered, together with many from abroad – especially the US and the rest of Europe – but audiences dwindled down to 238 million because money was short and people had more urgent priorities.

In 1932, the German cinema was full of fantasies. Lilian Harvey starred in *A Blonde's Dream,* in which her character wanted to be a film star in Hollywood but opted to stay at home because she was in love with a window cleaner (Willy Fritsch). Brigitte Helm played a film extra who, when threatened with the loss of her job, declared herself to be *The Countess of Monte Christo.* Lien Dyers was on the way from being a post-office clerk to becoming a film star in the comedy *The Company's in Love,* but ended up merely celebrating her engagement to Gustav Fröhlich with a trip to Venice. Jenny Jugo happened to fall bottom first onto the drums of the *Five of the Jazzband,* but finished up not with a musician but with a rich husband instead. Dolly Haas, daughter of a rich board director, ran over the unemployed Heinz Rühmann, and thus met the love of her life in a film called *Things Are Getting Better Already.*

In the musical *I By Day and You By Night* (p. 272), the Comedian Harmonists sang a song with the following lyrics:

> *I watch my Sunday film and sigh,*
> *As violins play up in the sky;*
> *On Monday morning I still dream:*
> *If only one day that was me,*
> *But such a thing could never be.*

In the film, nevertheless, Käthe von Nagy as the manicurist Grete and Willy Fritsch as the waiter Hans do find a happy ending together – inside a cinema.

At the end of *Whither Germany?* (p. 270), a passenger on the Berlin underground asks: 'Who will change the world?' Another replies: 'Those who are not satisfied.' Sadly, the following months proved this statement to be true in ways that its author, Bertolt Brecht, would never have wished.

The End

The last movie premiere of the Weimar Republic was held on 21 March 1933 in Leipzig for *The Flower of Hawaii.* The film's Jewish director, Richard Oswald, emigrated in the same year to Vienna. Its Jewish composer, Paul Abraham, emigrated to Budapest. Its leading lady, Martha Eggerth, had one Jewish parent, and also emigrated to Vienna. Its distribution company, Aafa-Film, had Jewish owners, and was made bankrupt. A happy ending did not materialize for many of those involved in making the film, and the day after the premiere, the Reichstag passed the 'Enabling Act' suspending the Weimar Constitution. And that was the end of the Weimar Republic.

Was this a 'golden age'? Of course, there must be an element of doubt, bearing in mind what followed – the radical changes, the terrible losses, and the murderous Nazi racism that caused them. But when we think of the creative talents of the directors, authors, cameramen, set and costume designers, producers, actors and actresses involved in so many great films over those fourteen years, the concept of a golden age is not such a strange one. The number of Jewish contributors to this creative flowering was also extremely high, as indeed it was in the realms of art and culture generally. This fact is surely apparent from the biographical information on their origins and their exiles. We can only bow our heads in awe and respect before their artistic talent and their personal sufferings.

A few years from now, the 100th anniversary of the Weimar Republic will be celebrated. This great age of German cinema has long gone, but its leading lights are still recognized by historians of film and culture. And ironically, we can now see more films from that era than at any other time in the past. This is made possible by DVDs that make film history available to all of us. We can see the futuristic visions of *Metropolis*, the everyday lives of *People on Sunday*, the decadence of *The Blue Angel*, and life in the tent city in *Whither Germany?* Whether it is to the gambling dens of *Dr Mabuse*, the Hotel Atlantic of *The Last Laugh*, the *Joyless Street* or *The Cabinet of Dr Caligari*, there are always more voyages of discovery to be made.

Posters for *A Blonde's Dream* (1932) and *The Countess of Monte Christo* (1932).

The Films

in chronological order

Carmen
Gypsy Blood

Classic drama of jealousy with a tragic ending. Carmen, who works in a cigarette factory, quarrels with one of her fellow workers, is arrested, seduces José, the officer of the dragoons who is supposed to be guarding her, gets involved in a smuggling ring, and leads José off the straight and narrow. In the end, when she shows too much interest in the toreador Escamillo, José kills her. The story stays close to Mérimée's original novella, and music from Bizet's opera was played at the premiere. On 20 December 1918, the date of the world premiere, the Congress of Workers' and Soldiers' Councils met in Berlin and agreed on elections for a German National Assembly. The mood on the streets was verging on civil war.

Cast

Pola Negri	Carmen
Harry Liedtke	Don José Navarro
Leopold von Ledebur	Escamillo
Grete Diercks	Dolores, Don José's fiancée
Paul Biensfeldt	Garcia, smuggler
Paul Conradi	Dancaire, smuggler
Max Kronert	Remendado, smuggler
Margarete Kupfer	Carmen's landlady
Wilhelm Diegelmann	Prison guard
Magnus Stifter	Lieutenant Esteban

Director
Ernst Lubitsch
Screenplay
Hanns Kräly
Norbert Falk
based on the novella
by Prosper Mérimée
Cinematography
Alfred Hansen
Sets
Kurt Richter
Costumes
Ali Hubert
Music
Artur Vieregg
Production company
Projektions-AG Union,
Berlin
Producer
Paul Davidson
Premiere
20 December 1918, Berlin
Length
1,784 m, approx. 66 min.
Format
35 mm, b/w, silent

The seductive Carmen (Pola Negri) is hired to dance for the company of dragoons.

Above: Carmen (Pola Negri, right foreground) escapes from the dragoons who have arrested her.

Below: A besotted Don José (Harry Liedtke) comes to meet Carmen at the tavern of Lillas Pastia (Fritz Richard).

Pola Negri as Carmen and Harry Liedtke as Don José.

Above: While hiding among the smugglers, Don José is wounded in a dragoon attack and cared for by Carmen.
Below: Carmen dies at the hands of the jealous Don José.

1919

Die Austernprinzessin

The Oyster Princess

A satirical fairy tale about the cultural differences between Europe and America. The happy ending, in which the daughter of the rich American 'Oyster King' is united with the impoverished Prince Nucki, is accompanied by an outbreak of passionate foxtrotting. 'I remember a piece of business which caused a lot of comment at the time. A poor man had to wait in the magnificent entrance hall of the home of a multimillionaire. The parquet floor of the multimillionaire's home was of a most complicated design. The poor man in order to overcome his impatience and his humiliation after having waited for hours walked along the outlines of the very intricate pattern on the floor... it was the first time I turned from comedy to satire' (Ernst Lubitsch, 1947).

Cast

Victor Janson	Mr Quaker, Oyster King of America
Ossi Oswalda	Ossi, his daughter
Harry Liedtke	Prince Nucki
Julius Falkenstein	Josef, Nucki's friend
Max Kronert	Seligsohn the matchmaker
Curt Bois	Conductor
Gerhard Ritterband	Kitchen boy

Director
Ernst Lubitsch
Screenplay
Ernst Lubitsch
Hanns Kräly
Cinematography
Theodor Sparkuhl
Sets
Kurt Richter
Production company
Projektions-AG Union, Berlin
Producer
Paul Davidson
Premiere
20 June 1919, Berlin
Length
1,144 m, approx. 47 min.
Format
35 mm, b/w, silent

Josef (Julius Falkenstein) paces along the lines of the parquet floor in the Oyster King's hall.

Above: The father of Ossi (Ossi Oswalda) spies through her keyhole on the night of her wedding to Prince Nucki (Harry Liedtke).
Below: Harry Liedtke and Ossi Oswalda as the happy couple.

1919

Madame Dubarry

Passion

A French milliner's maid rises to be mistress of King Louis XV, but falls in the turmoil of
the French Revolution. Lubitsch's first historical film is poor history but great cinema,
with history given a personal slant and an ironic commentary. The French found
this German view of their past irritatingly un-Prussian. 'This film has a certain tone,
atmosphere, style. There is something about it that is reminiscent of Danton's Death,
and of Diary of a Hangman. Of gentle gavottes and pastoral plays. Of the guillotine and
the scaffold. Of counts and sans-culottes. Of arsonists and the surreal hiss of the falling
blade. Of blind man's buff being played on a volcano' (Bobby E. Lüthge, 1919).

Cast

Pola Negri	Jeanne Vaubernier, later Madame Dubarry
Emil Jannings	King Louis XV
Reinhold Schünzel	Minister Choiseul
Harry Liedtke	Armand de Foix
Eduard von Winterstein	Jean Dubarry
Karl Platen	Guillaume Dubarry
Paul Biensfeldt	Lebel, valet to the King
Magnus Stifter	Don Diego, Spanish envoy
Willy Kaiser-Heyl	Commander of the watch
Elsa Berna	Duchesse de Gramont
Fred Immler	Comte de Richelieu
Marga Köhler	Madame Labille
Bernhard Goetzke	Revolutionary

Director
Ernst Lubitsch
Screenplay
Hanns Kräly
Norbert Falk
Cinematography
Theodor Sparkuhl
Sets
Kurt Richter
Costumes
Ali Hubert
Music
Alexander Schirmann
Production company
Projektions-AG Union,
Berlin
Producer
Paul Davidson
Premiere
18 September 1919, Berlin
Length
2,493 m, approx. 82 min.
Format
35 mm, tinted, silent

King Louis XV (Emil Jannings) plays blind man's buff with his courtiers.

Pola Negri as Madame Dubarry.

Madame Dubarry (Pola Negri) becomes the mistress of King Louis XV (Emil Jannings).

Above: Madame Dubarry (Pola Negri) begs her former lover Armand (Harry Liedtke) for mercy, but to no avail.
Below: Madame Dubarry faces the guillotine.

Rose Bernd

The Sins of Rose Bernd

A tragic drama about a woman who has the best of intentions but is brought to ruin by blackmail and rape, and eventually kills her own child. The film is based on a play by Gerhart Hauptmann, and is based on a real-life court case for which the author served as a juror. 'When in the film Rose Bernd is seduced by the landowner Flamm and then by the sadistic Streckmann, the details are revealed all the more vividly (a moralist would say "painfully"). Why? Because in the theatre the words have to be so restrained that they somehow conceal the totally sensuous actions – the words divert attention from them. In the cinema, the actions speak directly for themselves. Every movement can be seen so much more clearly' (Alfred Kerr, 1921).

Cast

Henny Porten	Rose Bernd
Alexander Wierth	Christoph Flamm
Emil Jannings	Arthur Streckmann
Paul Bildt	August Keil, bookseller
Ilka Grüning	Frau Flamm
Werner Krauss	Rose's father
Rigmore Törsleff	Martell, Rose's sister
Rudolf Biebrach	Magistrate

Director
Alfred Halm
Screenplay
Alfred Halm
based on the play by
Gerhart Hauptmann
Cinematography
Willibald Gaebel
Sets
Hans Baluschek
Music
Giuseppe Becce
Production company
Messter-Film GmbH, Berlin
Producer
Oskar Messter
Premiere
5 October 1919, Berlin
Length
1,900 m, approx. 70 min.
Format
35 mm, b/w, silent

Rose Bernd (Henny Porten) becomes the mistress of the married Flamm (Alexander Wierth).

Maud (Mia May) is reunited with her long-lost son (Ernst Hofmann).

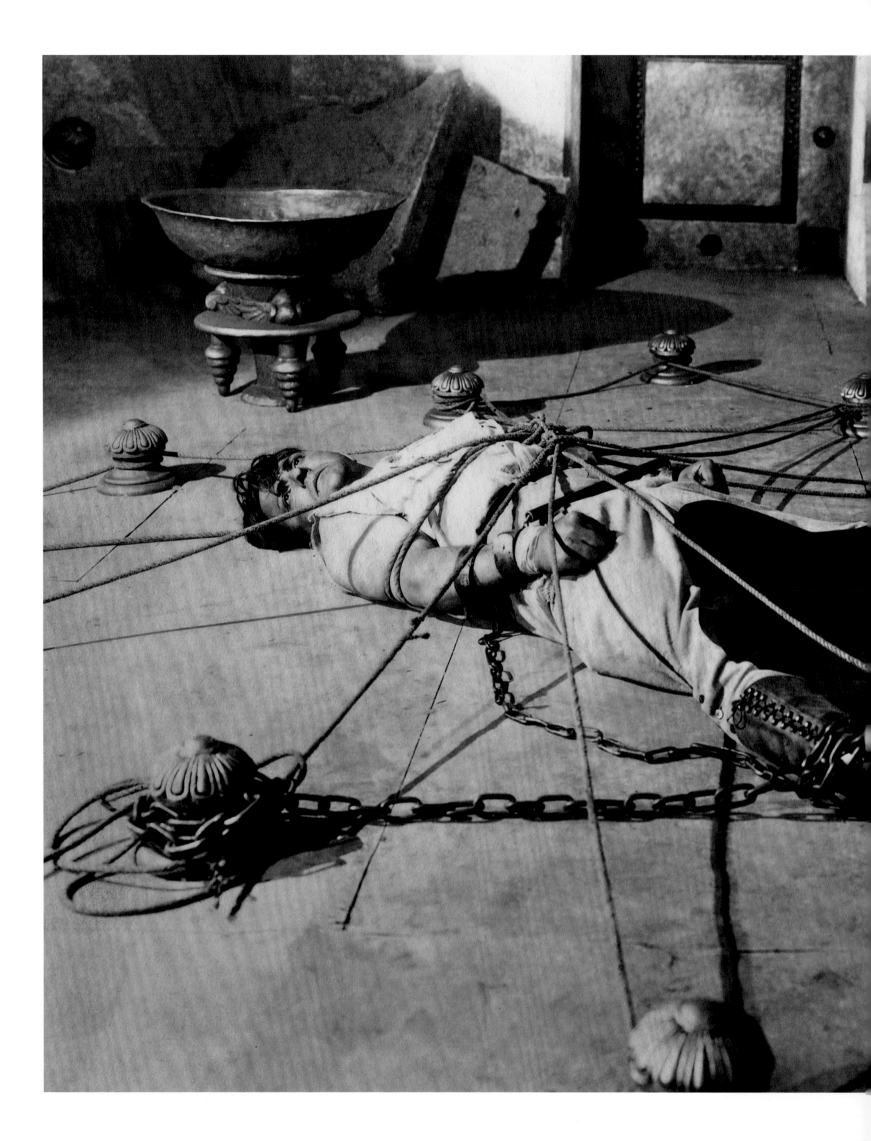

Michael Bohnen as Holger Madsen in a scene of peril.

Das Cabinet des Dr. Caligari

The Cabinet of Dr Caligari

Caligari, a showman, hypnotizes the sleepwalker Cesare and forces him to commit a string of murders. The frame story is set in a lunatic asylum, in which Dr Caligari is the director. 'Almost every image is a success: the little town on a mountain (all the sets are painted, and nothing is acted before anything real), a square with carousels, strange rooms, beautifully stylized offices in which Hoffmannesque clerks perch on angular stools and give their orders. The mime is complex, the interplay of light and shadow on the walls is intricate. The tale of the victimized sleepwalker is nothing new – but it is memorably told. Many images stick in the mind: the murderer in his lofty cell, streets with running people, a dark alley – to come up with all those things requires a belief in miracles' (Kurt Tucholsky, 1920).

Cast

Werner Krauss	Dr Caligari
Conrad Veidt	Cesare the somnambulist
Friedrich Fehér	Francis
Lil Dagover	Jane Olsen
Hans Heinrich von Twardowski	Alan
Rudolf Lettinger	Dr Olsen
Ludwig Rex	Murderer
Elsa Wagner	Landlady
Henri Peters-Arnolds	Young doctor
Hans Lander-Rudolf	Old man
Rudolf Klein-Rogge	Criminal

Director
Robert Wiene
Screenplay
Carl Mayer
Hans Janowitz
Cinematography
Willy Hameister
Sets
Hermann Warm
Walter Reimann
Walter Röhrig
Costumes
Walter Reimann
Music
Giuseppe Becce
Production company
Decla-Film-Ges.
Holz & Co, Berlin
Producers
Erich Pommer
Rudolf Meinert
Premiere
26 February 1920, Berlin
Length
1,780 m, approx. 75 min.
Format
35 mm, b/w, tinted, silent

Dr Caligari (Werner Krauss) presents Cesare the somnambulist to the crowd at a travelling fair.

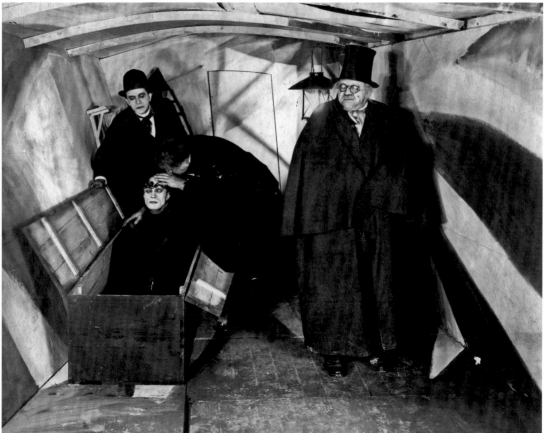

Above: Caligari (Werner Krauss, left) waits to ask the town clerk for a licence to perform at the fair.

Below: Caligari allows Francis (Friedrich Fehér) and Dr Olsen (Rudolf Lettinger) to examine the sleeping body of Cesare (Conrad Veidt).

Cesare (Conrad Veidt) attacks the sleeping Jane (Lil Dagover).

Pursued by the townspeople, Cesare (Conrad Veidt) drops the captive Jane (Lil Dagover) and escapes.

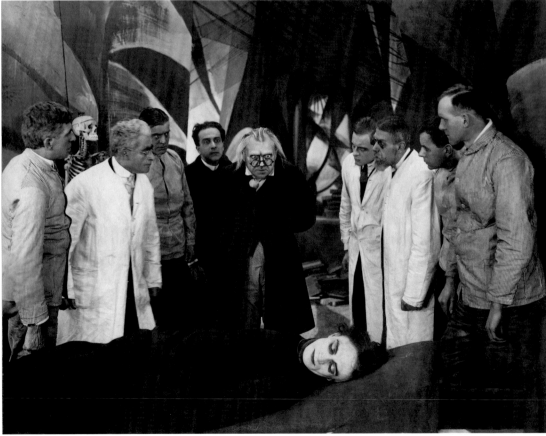

Above: Francis and Dr Olsen find the distraught Jane at home after her kidnapping.
Below: Caligari (centre) goes into shock on seeing the dead body of Cesare.

1920

Kohlhiesels Töchter
Kohlhiesel's Daughters

The innkeeper Kohlhiesel has two daughters: the rude, argumentative Liesel and the kind, friendly Gretel. The younger Gretel is not allowed to get married until Liesel has found a husband. This becomes a life-changing experience for the character played by Jannings. 'Henny Porten as the two daughters is a gag that is pure cinema, and playing with appearances is pure Lubitsch. It remains unclear whether it is an intentional effect that Henny Porten, when she should be herself, is an absolute shrew, and when she plays the shrew, she delights even the spectator with the charm to which eventually Jannings has to succumb' (Frieda Grafe, 1979).

Cast
Jakob Tiedtke — Mathias Kohlhiesel
Henny Porten — Gretel/Liesel
Emil Jannings — Peter Xaver
Gustav von Wangenheim — Paul Seppl
Willi Prager — Seidenstock the pedlar

Director
Ernst Lubitsch
Screenplay
Hanns Kräly
Ernst Lubitsch
Cinematography
Theodor Sparkuhl
Sets
Jack Winter
Costumes
Jan Baluschek
Music
Giuseppe Becce
Production company
Messter-Film GmbH, Berlin
Producer
Oskar Messter
Premiere
9 March 1920, Berlin
Length
1,129 m, approx. 41 min.
Format
35 mm, b/w, silent

Henny Porten in the dual role of sisters Gretel and Liesel.

Above: Seppl (Gustav von Wangenheim) and Liesel (Henny Porten) come up with a plan to improve both of their lives.
Below: Liesel hides from the feigned rage of her unwilling husband Xaver (Emil Jannings).

Der Golem, wie er in die Welt kam
The Golem

This was the second version of the Golem story to be filmed by Wegener. What the architect Hans Poelzig constructed on Ufa's Tempelhof site was not medieval Prague but an Expressionist realm. The Jewish legend of the Golem was combined with German Romanticism and Wegener's own cinematic fantasy world. 'The scene of the appeal to the demon with its circles of flames is even more poignant than the corresponding scene in Murnau's Faust: the demon's phosphorescent head, with its sad, empty eyes, is suddenly transformed into a huge Chinese mask looming up in profile at the edge of the screen with a kind of prodigious ferocity' (Lotte H. Eisner, 1955).

Cast
Paul Wegener — The Golem
Albert Steinrück — Rabbi Loew
Lyda Salmonova — Miriam, Rabbi Loew's daughter
Ernst Deutsch — Famulus
Otto Gebühr — Emperor Rudolf II
Lothar Müthel — Sir Florian
Loni Nest — Little girl
Hans Sturm — Chief Rabbi
Max Kronert — Gatekeeper
Greta Schröder — Rose maiden

Directors
Paul Wegener
Carl Boese
Screenplay
Paul Wegener
Henrik Galeen
Cinematography
Karl Freund
Sets
Hans Poelzig
Costumes
Rochus Gliese
Music
Hans Landsberger
Production company
Projektions-AG Union, Berlin
Producer
Paul Davidson
Premiere
29 October 1920, Berlin
Length
1,922 m, approx. 86 min.
Format
35 mm, b/w, silent

The Golem (Paul Wegener, centre) is taken to the Emperor's court for the Rose Festival.

The people of the Prague ghetto rush to the street to hear the news of the Golem's rampage.

A publicity still shows the Golem (Paul Wegener) looming over the Prague ghetto.

Above: Courtiers beg the Golem (Paul Wegener) for help as the palace begins to collapse around them.
Below: Rabbi Loew (Albert Steinrück) gives thanks to God as he stands over the Golem's lifeless body.

Anna Boleyn

Anne Boleyn

Lubitsch's second costume drama, based on 16th-century British history: a lady-in-waiting rises to become Henry VIII's second wife. But Henry turns away from Anne when she can only produce a daughter, and she is eventually accused of adultery and beheaded. This is no comedy. 'The buildings alone gave employment to 14 site foremen, 200 carpenters, 400 plasterers, sculptors, etc. The historically accurate copy of Westminster Abbey required 380 sculptures, while 500 horses and 4,000 riders and spectators were required for a tournament scene. Miss Henny Porten had to have sixteen costumes, and Mr Jannings ten' (Lichtbild-Bühne, 1920). The production cost around 8 million marks. Ticket sales in the US alone, however, brought in $200,000, almost double those costs.

Cast

Henny Porten	Anne Boleyn
Emil Jannings	Henry VIII
Hedwig Pauly-Winterstein	Queen Catherine
Hilde Müller	Princess Mary
Ludwig Hartau	Duke of Norfolk
Aud Egede Nissen	Jane Seymour
Ferdinand von Alten	Mark Smeaton
Paul Hartmann	Sir Henry Norris
Maria Reisenhofer	Lady Rochford
Adolf Klein	Cardinal Wolsey
Paul Biensfeldt	Jester

Director
Ernst Lubitsch
Screenplay
Norbert Falk
Hanns Kräly
Cinematography
Theodor Sparkuhl
Sets
Kurt Richter
Costume
Ali Hubert
Music
Hans Landsberger
Production company
Messter-Film GmbH, Berlin
Projektions-AG Union,
Berlin
Producer
Paul Davidson
Premiere
3 December 1920, Weimar
Length
2,793 m, approx. 103 min.
Format
35 mm, b/w, silent

Aud Egede Nissen as Jane Seymour, Emil Jannings as Henry VIII and Henny Porten as Anne Boleyn.

Anne (Henny Porten) is accused of adultery and sent to the Tower of London.

1921

Hamlet

A revenge drama with only a small debt to Shakespeare's play. When the Danish king and queen produce a daughter instead of a hoped-for son and heir, they keep it a closely guarded secret and bring up the child as a boy. This gives a novel twist to the traditional tale, but Asta Nielsen rises to the stature of a prince. 'Nielsen as Hamlet never tries to hide from the audience the fact that she is a young woman who has enjoyed being brought up as a prince. She has the aristocratic bearing and the freedom of movement, but these are always measured and played down. No gesture is artificial, no movement seems forced, with too abrupt a beginning or ending. This character is filled with a nobility that is deep seated or that gradually becomes so' (Thomas Koebner, 1995).

Cast

Asta Nielsen	Prince Hamlet
Paul Conradi	King Hamlet of Denmark
Mathilde Brandt	Queen Gertrude
Eduard von Winterstein	Claudius
Heinz Stieda	Horatio
Hans Junkermann	Polonius
Anton de Verdier	Laertes
Lily Jacobsson	Ophelia
Fritz Achterberg	King Fortinbras of Norway

Director
Svend Gade
Heinz Schall
Screenplay
Erwin Gepard
based on the medieval
saga of Hamlet
Cinematography
Curt Courant
Axel Graatkjaer
Sets
Siegfried Wroblewski
Svend Gade
Costumes
Hugo Baruch
Leopold Verch
Production company
Art-Film GmbH, Berlin
Producer
Asta Nielsen
Premiere
4 February 1921, Berlin
Length
2,367 m, approx. 110 min.
Format
35 mm, b/w, silent

Claudius (Eduard von Winterstein, right) orders the suspicious Hamlet (Asta Nielsen) to go to Norway with Rosencrantz and Guildenstern.

Hamlet (Asta Nielsen) is spurred on to revenge by a dream of her dead father.

Hamlet's task is complicated by her secret love of Horatio, who himself is in love with Ophelia.

After the death of Hamlet, Fortinbras (Fritz Achterberg, far right) takes the throne.

Die Bergkatze

The Wildcat

Comedy about the wild daughter of a bandit chief who falls for a soldier from the local fort. This was one of Lubitsch's few flops, although it does feature a rather spectacular firework display. With this satire on militarism and war, Lubitsch evidently misjudged the spirit of the times, as German audiences were not yet ready to laugh at the sight of comical soldiers trudging theatrically through the snow.

Cast

Pola Negri	Rischka the 'Wildcat'
Victor Janson	Fort Commander
Paul Heidemann	Lieutenant Alexis
Wilhelm Diegelmann	Claudius the bandit chief
Hermann Thimig	Pepo the bandit
Edith Mellern	Lilli, the Fort Commander's daughter
Marga Köhler	Fort Commander's wife
Paul Biensfeldt	Dafko the bandit
Paul Graetz	Zofano the bandit
Max Kronert	Masilio the bandit
Erwin Kopp	Tripo the bandit

Director
Ernst Lubitsch
Screenplay
Hanns Kräly
Ernst Lubitsch
Cinematography
Theodor Sparkuhl
Sets
Ernst Stern
Costumes
Ernst Stern
Production company
Projektions-AG Union, Berlin
Producer
Paul Davidson
Premiere
12 April 1921, Berlin
Length
1,818 m, approx. 67 min.
Format
35 mm, b/w and tinted, silent

Rischka (Pola Negri) and her bandit gang sneak into the fort, under the nose of its commander (Victor Janson, centre).

Above and below: Pola Negri as the rebellious Rischka and Paul Heidemann as the prim Lieutenant Alexis.

Above and opposite: Rischka dresses up in the glamorous clothes of the fort commander's daughter.

Der müde Tod

Destiny / Between Two Worlds

A German folksong: four tales that ask whether love is stronger than death. Death gives a young woman three chances to save her beloved's life. Three times, in stories set in Persia, Renaissance Venice and China, she fails. 'Only when she is dead – after sacrificing her own life in order to save a child from a fire – can Death reunite her with her sweetheart. Now the wall opens up for the dead girl as for the dreamer, but this time it is for good. Making a film means seeing Death at work. Or seeing life turn into history, which amounts to the same thing' (Enno Patalas, 1976).

Cast

Bernhard Goetzke	Death/El Mot/Archer
Lil Dagover	Young woman/Zobeide/
	Fiametta/Tiao Tsien
Walter Janssen	Young man/Franke/
	Giovanfrancesco/Liang
Max Adalbert	Notary/Chancellor
Wilhelm Diegelmann	Doctor
Hans Sternberg	Mayor
Ernst Rückert	Priest
Erich Pabst	Teacher
Karl Platen	Apothecary
Rudolf Klein-Rogge	Dervish/Girolamo
Eduard von Winterstein	Caliph
Lothar Müthel	Messenger
Louis Brody	Moor

Director
Fritz Lang
Screenplay
Thea von Harbou
Fritz Lang
Cinematography
Fritz Arno Wagner
Erich Nitzschmann
Hermann Saalfrank
Sets
Walter Röhrig
Hermann Warm
Robert Herlth
Costumes
Heinrich Umlauff
Music
Giuseppe Becce
Production company
Decla-Bioscop AG, Berlin
Producer
Erich Pommer
Premiere
6 October 1921, Berlin
Length
2,307 m, approx. 99 min.
Format
35 mm, b/w, silent

At the film's climax, Lil Dagover saves a child's life by giving herself over to Death (Bernhard Goetzke).

Above and below: In the Venice segment, the lovers are betrayed when their messenger (Lothar Müthel) is killed.

Death (Bernhard Goetzke) takes his victims behind a vast wall of stone.

1921

Hintertreppe
Backstairs

Three people are embroiled in a dark tale of jealousy: a maid, her lover and a postman. Only the postman survives. 'The eerily sad and dingy backstairs world between courtyards, passages and doorways, masterfully recreated by Jessner; the other human world – that of the light, of the façade of life – is glimpsed only collectively, only anonymously. The whole thing is perfect. I sat there, initially nodding in admiration, but then simply living and suffering with the characters, completely absorbed and captivated' (Bruno Frank, 1921).

Cast
Henny Porten — Maid
Wilhelm Dieterle — Workman
Fritz Kortner — Postman

Directors
Leopold Jessner
(performance direction)
Paul Leni (art direction)
Screenplay
Carl Mayer
Cinematography
Karl Hasselmann
Sets
Paul Leni
Music
Hans Landsberger
Production company
Henny Porten-Film GmbH, Berlin
Producers
Hanns Lippmann
Henny Porten
Premiere
11 December 1921
Length
1,339 m, approx. 49 min.
Format
35 mm, b/w, silent

The maid (Henny Porten) is distraught when she finds out that a letter from her lover was forged by the postman who secretly loves her (Fritz Kortner).

The postman (Fritz Kortner) murders his rival in love (Wilhelm Dieterle).

1922

Nosferatu. Eine Symphonie des Grauens
Nosferatu: A Symphony of Horror

A classic tale of terror, adapted from Bram Stoker's <u>Dracula</u> but with the names changed in an unsuccessful attempt to avoid accusations of copyright infringement. 'Shivery anxiety and nightmares, shadowy forms and premonitions of death, madness and ghosts were all woven into the images of gloomy mountainous landscapes and stormy seas. There was also a ghostly coach ride through the forest which was neither supernatural nor gruesome. But the nature images were overlaid with premonitions of the supernatural. Storm clouds scurrying in front of the moon, a ruin by night, a dark, unidentifiable silhouette in the empty courtyard, a spider on a human face, the ship with black sails sailing along the canal without anyone in sight to steer it, howling wolves in the night and horses suddenly shying without our knowing why – all these images are perfectly possible in nature. But they were surrounded by an icy blast from another world. What is certain is that no written or oral literature is able to express the ghostly, the demonic and the supernatural as well as the cinema' (Béla Balász, 1924).

Cast

Max Schreck	Count Orlok
Alexander Granach	Knock
Gustav von Wangenheim	Thomas Hutter
Greta Schröder	Ellen Hutter
Georg Heinrich Schnell	Reeder Harding
Ruth Landshoff	Ruth, his sister
John Gottowt	Professor Bulwer
Gustav Botz	Professor Sievers
Max Nemetz	Captain
Wolfgang Heinz	Ship's mate
Albert Venohr	Sailor
Guido Herzfeld	Landlord

Director
F. W. Murnau
Screenplay
Henrik Galeen
based on the novel
by Bram Stoker
Cinematography
Fritz Arno Wagner
Sets
Albin Grau
Costumes
Albin Grau
Music
Hans Erdmann
Production company
Prana-Film GmbH, Berlin
Producers
Albin Grau
Enrico Dieckmann
Premiere
4 March 1922, Berlin
Length
1,967 m, approx. 94 min.
Format
35 mm, tinted, silent

Count Orlok (Max Schreck) is fascinated by a portrait of Ellen, the fiancée of Thomas Hutter (Gustav von Wangenheim).

Rudolf Klein-Rogge in some of Mabuse's many guises

Dr. Mabuse, der Spieler

Wenk (Bernhard Goetzke) takes Mabuse's henchman Pesch (Georg John) to confront
Cara Carozza (Aud Egede Nissen) but finds she has committed suicide on Mabuse's orders.

Lucrezia Borgia

Historical drama. The villain is Cesare Borgia, who is riddled with hatred, jealousy and passion. Even banishment by his father, Pope Alexander VI, cannot stop him. Lucrezia, who is his cousin in this version of the story, flees his unwanted advances and seeks refuge in the castle of the Sforzas, where Cesare is killed in a duel. The finale of this lavish production was filmed on the Tempelhof site.

Cast

Liane Haid	Lucrezia Borgia
Conrad Veidt	Cesare Borgia
Albert Bassermann	Pope Alexander VI
Paul Wegener	Micheletto
Heinrich George	Sebastiano
Adolf Edgar Licho	Lodovico
Wilhelm Dieterle	Giovanni Sforza
Lothar Müthel	Juan Borgia
Käte Oswald	Naomi
Alexander Granach	Jailor
Anita Berber	Countess Julia Orsini

Director
Richard Oswald
Screenplay
Richard Oswald
based on the novel
by Harry Scheff
Cinematography
Karl Freund
Sets
Robert Neppach
Botho Höfer
Costumes
Robert Neppach
Production company
Richard Oswald-Film AG,
Berlin
Producer
Richard Oswald
Premiere
20 October 1922, Berlin
Length
3,284 m, approx. 75 min.
Format
35 mm, b/w, silent

Cesare Borgia (Conrad Veidt) threatens to kill the fiancé of his cousin Lucrezia (Liane Haid).

Banished by his father, the Pope, Cesare (Conrad Veidt) begs Lucrezia (Liane Haid) for mercy.

Ein Glas Wasser

A Glass of Water

Comedy. Romantic intrigues at the English royal court, between Queen Anne, little Lieutenant Masham, the Duchess of Marlborough and the middle-class Abigail. Political and state affairs as presented by Eugène Scribe, who wrote the original play, remain very much in the background. 'Without losing anything of the charming light-heartedness of the so perfectly written, much performed play, Ludwig Berger gives new depth to this merry light comedy of French provenance. The intrigue itself is expanded to offer a deeper meaning, and the victory of good over evil takes on an allegorical significance that is reminiscent of folk tales, Mozart operas and late Shakespeare' (Rudolf Freund, 1988).

Cast

Mady Christians	Queen Anne
Helga Thomas	Abigail
Hans Brausewetter	Masham
Lucie Höflich	Duchess of Marlborough
Rudolf Rittner	Lord Henry of Bolingbroke
Hans Wassmann	Lord Richard Scott
Bruno Decarli	Marquis de Torcy
Hugo Döblin	Tomwood
Max Gülstorff	Thompson

Director
Ludwig Berger
Screenplay
Ludwig Berger
Adolf Lantz
based on the play
by Eugène Scribe
Cinematography
Günther Krampf
Erich Waschneck
Sets
Rudolf Bamberger
Hermann Warm
Costumes
Otto Schulz (men)
Karl Töpfer (women)
Music
Bruno Schulz
Production company
Decla-Bioscop AG, Berlin
Producer
Erich Pommer
Premiere
1 February 1923, Berlin
Length
2,558 m, approx. 94 min.
Format
35 mm, b/w, silent

Helga Thomas as Abigail and Mady Christians as Queen Anne.

Lucie Höflich as the Duchess of Marlborough.

1923

Buddenbrooks

In Gerhard Lamprecht's film adaptation of Thomas Mann's novel, the main focus is on the fate of Thomas Buddenbrook, the youngest son of the patrician Lübeck family. Five years later, Mann distanced himself from the film with a general criticism: 'Instead of narrating, always simply narrating and letting the characters live their lives, they have turned it into a mediocre merchant's tragedy, and they have left practically nothing of the novel except the characters' names' (1928). The author had strong views on everything, including cinematic matters, but he did not do justice to this, the first film version.

Cast

Peter Esser	Thomas Buddenbrook
Mady Christians	Gerda Arnoldsen
Alfred Abel	Christian Buddenbrook
Hildegard Imhof	Tony Buddenbrook
Mathilde Sussin	Elisabeth Buddenbrook
Franz Egénieff	Reeder Arnoldsen
Ralph Arthur Roberts	Bendix Grünlich
Charlotte Böcklin	Aline Puvogel
Karl Platen	Marcus the lawyer
Kurt Vespermann	Renee Throta
Elsa Wagner	Sesemi Weichbrodt

Director
Gerhard Lamprecht
Screenplay
Alfred Fekete
Luise Heilborn-Körbitz
based on the novel
by Thomas Mann
Cinematography
Erich Waschneck
Herbert Stephan
Sets
Otto Moldenhauer
Music
Giuseppe Becce
Production company
Dea-Film GmbH, Berlin
Producer
Albert Pommer
Premiere
31 August 1923, Berlin
Length
2,383 m, approx. 90 min.
Format
35 mm, b/w, silent

The elegant home of the Buddenbrook family.

Above: Auguste Prasch-Grevenberg, Franz Egénieff, Alfred Abel, Rudolf del Zopp, Peter Esser (standing), Mady Christians, Mathilde Sussin and Hildegard Imhof.
Below: Mady Christians, Mathilde Sussin and Franz Egénieff.

1923

Schatten
Warning Shadows

Subtitled 'A Nocturnal Hallucination'. At an evening party, the guests are hypnotized by a shadow play, but the host is driven mad with jealousy. The story was based on an idea by Albin Grau. 'The old interplay between appearance and reality, in which appearance tells us more than everyday life about reality, which for the most part is hidden behind a façade. In the 1920s, when the aim in the cinema was not yet to save the world but just to save a marriage, one was able to manage with comparatively simple tricks. Even though the director set up something quite confusing, Fritz Arno Wagner's camera turned the shadows into a great Expressionist experiment' (Peter Buchka, 1995).

Cast
Fritz Kortner — Husband
Ruth Weyher — Wife
Gustav von Wangenheim — Lover
Alexander Granach — Shadow-player
Eugen Rex — 1st gentleman
Max Gülstoff — 2nd gentleman
Ferdinand von Alten — 3rd gentleman
Fritz Rasp — 1st servant
Karl Platen — 2nd servant
Lilly Harder — Maid

Director
Arthur Robison
Screenplay
Rudolf Schneider
Arthur Robison
Cinematography
Fritz Arno Wagner
Sets
Albin Grau
Costumes
Albin Grau
Music
Ernst Riege
Production company
Pan-Film GmbH, Berlin
Producer
Enrico Dieckmann
Premiere
16 October 1923, Berlin
Length
1,710 m, approx. 85 min.
Format
35 mm, b/w, silent

Reflected in a mirror, Fritz Kortner (left) sees his wife (Ruth Weyher) bidding a passionate farewell to her lover (Gustav von Wangenheim).

Fritz Kortner's jealous rage becomes murderous.

Above: A servant (Karl Platen) witnesses a violent scene played out in shadow form.
Below: Ruth Weyher, Karl Platen and Fritz Rasp fall under the spell of the shadow play.

Ruth Weyher, menaced by shadows.

1923

Die Strasse
The Street

The film covers the events of a single night. One evening, a respectable, middle-class man leaves his wife in order to sample life in the big city; the next morning he ruefully goes back to her. This was an early example of the genre of the 'street film'. 'Grune's film establishes not only the subject but also the visual richness that remains typical of street films: the predilection for mid shots, showing people in the social milieu that defines and characterizes them; the flashes of light that pass through the window and illuminate the neat and tidy living room, promising that something exciting is about to happen; the swift changes of shot, suggesting hectic disorder; the decorative arrangement of the crowds, within which individual fates are interwoven with those of everyone else' (Norbert Grab, 2003).

Cast
Anton Edthofer — Pimp
Aud Egede Nissen — Prostitute
Eugen Klöpfer — Middle-class man
Lucie Höflich — Middle-class man's wife
Leonhard Haskel — Man from the provinces
Max Schreck — Blind man
Hans Trautner — Man

Director
Karl Grune
Screenplay
Karl Grune
Julius Urgiss
based on an idea
by Carl Mayer
Cinematography
Karl Hasselmann
Sets
Karl Görge
Ludwig Meidner
Production company
Stern-Film GmbH, Berlin
Producer
Karl Grune
Premiere
29 November 1923, Berlin
Length
2,057 m, approx. 90 min.
Format
35 mm, b/w, silent

The atmospheric street scenes were filmed on studio sets.

Eugen Klöpfer and Aud Egede Nissen below an optometrist's sign,
given a sinister slant by the surrounding darkness.

The nameless protagonist (Eugen Klöpfer) is lured away from his bourgeois world by the temptations of the city streets.

Aud Egede Nissen plays a prostitute, embodying the allure and danger of the city.

Sylvester

New Year's Eve

The tale of a night of tragedy. A café owner can no longer stand the constant bickering between his wife and his mother. On New Year's Eve, he commits suicide while everyone else is celebrating in the front room. A psychodrama in fifty-four scenes. 'For me, the essence of the film was not the psychological side (it seems to me, the longer it is, the more convincing it becomes, but such things belong in the novel or the theatre, not in a film, because a film needs not just internal but also and especially external movement, conflict, tempo) ...the essence was its mastery of the milieu; for the first time in film, here we had the pulsating life of the Earth's surface, remorselessly revealed in such breadth that the individual event became a symbol of this vastness' (Kurt Pinthus, 1924).

Cast
Edith Posca   Woman
Eugen Klöpfer   Man
Frida Richard   Mother
Karl Harbacher
Rudolf Blümner

Director
Lupu Pick
Screenplay
Carl Mayer
Cinematography
Karl Hasselmann
Guido Seeber
Sets
Klaus Richter
Music
Klaus Pringsheim
Production company
Rex-Film AG, Berlin
Producer
Lupu Pick
Premiere
3 January 1924
Length
1,529 m, approx. 56 min.
Format
35 mm, b/w, silent

The drama being played out indoors is intercut with scenes of New Year celebrations outside.

Above: Rudolf Blümner is among the revellers oblivious of the tragedy.

Below: Edith Posca and Frida Richard (in the background) are the wife and mother-in-law in constant conflict.

Die Nibelungen

A classic tale from German mythology in two parts: Siegfried's apprenticeship with the blacksmith Mime, the fight with the dragon, the defeat of Alberich, the capture of the Nibelung treasure and the magic helmet, the proposal of marriage to Kriemhild at the court of Worms, the wooing of Brunhild for King Gunther, the double wedding, the quarrel between the queens, and the murder of Siegfried by Hagen von Tronje (Part I: Siegfried). The sinking of the Nibelung treasure in the Rhine, Kriemhild's marriage to Etzel, the King of the Huns, the feast at the royal court that turns into a terrible scene of revenge, death and destruction (Part 2: Kriemhild's Revenge). The massacre at the end lasts for forty-five minutes. At the premiere, the final act could not be shown as the editing had not yet been completed.

Cast

Margarethe Schön	Kriemhild
Paul Richter	Siegfried
Hans Adalbert Schlettow	Hagen von Tronje
Bernhard Goetzke	Volker von Alzey
Hanna Ralph	Brunhild
Theodor Loos	King Gunther
Erwin Biswanger	Giselher
Georg John	Mime the blacksmith/
	Alberich the Nibelung
Gertrud Arnold	Queen Ute
Rudolf Klein-Rogge	King Etzel (Part 2)
Fritz Alberti	Dietrich von Bern (Part 2)

Director
Fritz Lang
Screenplay
Thea von Harbou
Cinematography
Carl Hoffmann
Günther Rittau
Stills photography
Horst von Harbou
Sets
Otto Hunte
Erich Kettelhut
Karl Vollbrecht
Costumes
Änne Willkomm
Music
Gottfried Huppertz
Production company
Decla-Bioscop AG, Berlin
Producer
Erich Pommer
Premiere
24 February 1924 (Part I)
26 April 1924 (Part 2)
Length
3,216 m (Part I),
approx. 118 min.
3,576 m (Part 2),
approx. 123 min.
Format
35 mm, b/w, silent

Siegfried (Paul Richter) forges his own sword.

Hans Adalbert Schlettow as the warrior Hagen.

The death of Siegfried (Paul Richter), at the hands of Hagen.

Michael

Heart's Desire / Chained: The Story of the Third Sex

A story of renunciation, based on a novel by Hermann Bang. The famous painter Zoret loses his beloved model, a young man called Michael, to the beautiful but penniless Princess Zamikoff. 'A film full of the thunder of approaching changes, just as art at the turn of the century was fundamentally affected by the intrusion of sexuality. This was not the homosexual, idealistic relationship between master and pupil, between classical painter and model. Now it is woman who returns to the scene. The youth turns his spiritual father's art into money for his extravagant sweetheart. Its complexity of expression makes the film impossible to pin down' (Frieda Grafe, 1974).

Cast

Walter Slezak	Eugène Michael
Benjamin Christensen	Claude Zoret
Nora Gregor	Princess Zamikoff
Alexander Murski	Herr Adelskjold
Grete Mosheim	Alice Adelskjold
Didier Aslan	Duke of Monthieu
Robert Garrison	Charles Swift, art critic
Max Auzinger	Butler
Karl Freund	Leblanc, art dealer

Director
Carl Theodor Dreyer
Screenplay
Thea von Harbou
Carl Theodor Dreyer
based on the novel
by Hermann Bang
Cinematography
Karl Freund
Rudolph Maté
Sets
Hugo Häring
Music
Hans Joseph Vieth
Production company
Decla-Bioscop AG,
Berlin, for Ufa
Producer
Erich Pommer
Premiere
26 September 1924, Berlin
Length
1,966 m, approx. 72 min.
Format
35 mm, b/w, silent

From left to right: Walter Slezak, Benjamin Christensen, Robert Garrison, Grete Mosheim, Alexander Murski and Max Auzinger.

Zoret (Benjamin Christensen, centre) welcomes the Duke of Monthieu (Didier Aslan) to his home, as his butler (Max Auzinger) looks on.

Das Wachsfigurenkabinett
Waxworks

Germany's three great character actors star as figures in a waxwork chamber of horrors: Jannings is Harun al-Rashid, Veidt is Ivan the Terrible and Krauss is Jack the Ripper. All three are products of the imagination of Wilhelm Dieterle, as a daydreaming poet who is asked to think up stories for the proprietor of the waxworks show. 'Leni reshapes the natural condition of things boldly and clearly into forms whose lines and surfaces anticipate the atmosphere of the scene. He inflates forms, then lets them shrink: in an oriental scene, he embellishes them in a most amusing way; in a Russian scene he smoothes them out in solemn, Byzantine fashion; and with his fingertips he feels the kinetic energy and powerful tensions of Expressionist decor in an uncanny sequence of scenes that gives a framework and form to Jack the Ripper' (Rudolf Kurtz, 1926).

Cast
Emil Jannings — Harun al-Rashid
Conrad Veidt — Ivan the Terrible
Werner Krauss — Jack the Ripper
Wilhelm Dieterle — Poet/Pastry baker/
Russian prince/Rinaldo
Rinaldini
Olga Belajeff — Eva/Maimune/Bojarin
John Gottowt — Waxworks proprietor
Paul Biensfeldt — Vizier

Directors
Paul Leni
Leo Birinski
(performance direction)
Screenplay
Henrik Galeen
Cinematography
Helmar Lerski
Sets
Paul Leni
Costumes
Ernst Stern
Production company
Neptun-Film AG,
Berlin, for Ufa
Premiere
6 October 1924
Length
2,142 m, approx. 83 min.
Format
35 mm, b/w, silent

Ivan the Terrible (Conrad Veidt, left) gazes in horror at an hourglass that counts out the seconds until his death by poison.

Four figures of fear: Emil Jannings as Harun al-Rashid, Conrad Veidt as Ivan the Terrible, Wilhelm Dieterle as Rinaldo Rinaldini
(whose story was cut from the final script) and Werner Krauss as Jack the Ripper.

Der letzte Mann
The Last Laugh

The tragicomic tale of an ageing hotel doorman who is demoted to the post of lavatory attendant, but does not dare to tell his relatives, friends or neighbours. The revolving door and the uniform are of central importance here, and the camera is more mobile than ever before. 'This doorman is anything but the still, silent servant who makes himself unobtrusive. On the contrary, he inflates himself to being the very symbol of the Grand Hotel; the lackey turns himself into the generalissimo, imposing himself on the world with his wide, imperious gestures. The Last Laugh truly reveals itself to be a film of inflation, for the world has gone off its hinges and the servant lays claim to the role of master. The perspectives adopted by the camera seem to place him on the imaginary hill of the field marshal. At its heart, this film is a satire on all rulers' (Karl Prümm, 2003).

Cast

Emil Jannings	Hotel doorman
Maly Delschaft	Niece
Max W. Hiller	Niece's fiancé
Emilie Kurz	Fiancé's aunt
Hans Unterkircher	Hotel manager
Olaf Storm	Young hotel guest
Hermann Vallentin	Pot-bellied guest
Georg John	Nightwatchman
Emmy Wyda	Neighbour

Director
F. W. Murnau
Screenplay
Carl Mayer
Cinematography
Karl Freund
Stills photography
Hans Natge
Sets
Robert Herlth
Walter Röhrig
Music
Giuseppe Becce
Production company
Union-Film der
Universum-Film, Berlin
Producer
Erich Pommer
Premiere
23 December 1924, Berlin
Length
2,315 m, approx. 90 min.
Format
35 mm, b/w, silent

The Hotel Atlantic provides the setting for the tale.

Emil Jannings (back to the camera) makes his way home.

Emil Jannings is distressed to find that someone else has taken over his job.

Above and below: Emil Jannings is reduced from the rank of doorman to the lowly status of lavatory attendant.

Zur Chronik von Grieshuus

The Chronicles of the Grey House

Drama. Two brothers are engaged in a life and death struggle over who is to inherit the Grey House, set on the moors of northern Germany in the 17th century. The building itself was designed by Hans Poelzig. 'There is the age-old village church, whose patron is the Lord of the Grey House: a perfectly integrated, organic whole uniting different styles, from the Gothic of the cemetery walls to the Baroque of the patron's carved wooden pulpit. We see the thatched cottages with their beehives and their sunflowers, and further out on the moors the junipers in bloom, filled with buzzing bees, and the Machandelboom, the mystic juniper tree of German fairytales from whose flames a magical bird flew out. Since olden times they have all been haunted by the ghosts of fratricide, infanticide and patricide' (Willy Haas, 1925).

Cast

Arthur Kraussneck	Master of the Grey House
Paul Hartmann	Hinrich
Rudolf Forster	Detlev
Rudolf Rittner	Owe Heiken
Lil Dagover	Bärbe
Gertrud Arnold	Matten
Gertrud Welcker	Gesine
Hans Peter Peterhans	Rolf

Director
Arthur von Gerlach
Screenplay
Thea von Harbou
based on the novel
by Theodor Storm
Cinematography
Fritz Arno Wagner
Carl Drews
Stills photography
Hans Natge
Sets
Robert Herlth
Walter Röhrig
Hans Poelzig
(building designs)
Costumes
Paul Gerd Guderian
Music
Gottfried Huppertz
Production company
Universum-Film AG (Ufa),
Berlin
Producer
Erich Pommer
Premiere
11 February 1925, Berlin
Length
2,966 m, approx. 109 min.
Format
35 mm, b/w, silent

Sheep on the Lüneburg Heath in northern Germany.

Paul Hartmann (on horseback) outside the Grey House, designed by architect Hans Poelzig.

One of the striking interior sets for the Grey House.

Ice skating was one of the sports featured, alongside boxing, tennis, gymnastics and the martial arts.

Die freudlose Gasse

Joyless Street

Cast

Asta Nielsen	Maria Lechner
Greta Garbo	Grete Rumfort
Agnes Esterhazy	Regina Rosenow
Werner Krauss	Master butcher
Henry Stuart	Egon Stirner
Einar Hanson	Lieutenant Davy
Ilka Grüning	Frau Rosenow
Jaro Fürth	Hofrat Rumfort
Robert Garrison	Don Alfonso Canez
Valeska Gert	Frau Greifer
Hertha von Walther	Else

Director
G. W. Pabst
Screenplay
Willy Haas
based on the novel
by Hugo Bettauer
Cinematography
Guido Seeber
Curt Oertel
Sets
Hans Sohnle
Otto Erdmann
Production company
Sofar-Film-Produktion
GmbH, Berlin
Producers
Michel Salkind
Romain Pinès
Premiere
18 May 1925, Berlin
Length
3,734 m, approx. 151 min.
Format
35 mm, b/w, silent

Vienna, 1925. Inflation has created social problems, and women in particular are suffering. The daughter of a civil servant loses her job, but is saved from prostitution by an American lieutenant; a young woman whose husband is unemployed is so desperate that she gives herself to a butcher; an old baron kills the wife of a lawyer – and watching over all this is Valeska Gert, who runs a nightclub and brothel where the women earn a little cash. Greta Garbo's only film in German. 'When we see Greta Garbo, the action comes almost to a standstill. Moments of sheer visual pleasure take over from narrative flow, and are staged as tableaux. Filmed in close-up and soft focus, Garbo becomes the object of the camera's masculine eye. When she is in front of the mirror, trying on the luxurious fur coat, the spectator becomes a voyeur whose perspective sits uneasily with the socially critical, New Objectivist style of the film' (Anton Kaes, 1993).

The butcher (Werner Krauss) with two streetwalkers.

Werner Krauss plays a corrupt butcher who promises meat to poor women in return for sexual favours.

Above: Driven to prostitution by poverty, Maria (Asta Nielsen) is propositioned by Don Alfonso (Robert Garrison).
Below: Watched by her sister Rosa (Loni Nest), Grete (Greta Garbo) tries on a fur coat in the boutique run by Frau Greifer (Valeska Gert).

Grete (Greta Garbo) is tempted by a coat from Frau Greifer (Valeska Gert), little knowing that her store is the front for a high-class brothel.

Die Verrufenen
Slums of Berlin

This film, based on the works of Heinrich Zille, captures a particular social environment. An engineer has spent some time in prison after committing perjury. When he is released, he finds there is no way back into society, has to seek refuge in a night shelter, considers suicide and is saved by a prostitute. 'The beauty of this film lies in its naturalism. We sit and admire scenes that we can see every day on the streets but which now become works of art – an astonishing experience. If one of us had to plan something on the subject of "social destitution", what would we think of? Dark and narrow alleyways, haggard Kollwitz figures, their faces decorated with lines of suffering… but here we see how an artist can extract powerful effects from reality, and blow Zille's air into the nostrils of the public' (Rudolf Arnheim, 1925).

Cast

Bernhard Goetzke	Robert Kramer
Paul Bildt	Kramer's father
Margarete Kupfer	Housekeeper
Aud Egede Nissen	Emma
Arthur Bergen	Gustav
Eduard Rothauser	Rottmann
Mady Christians	Regine Lossen
Aribert Wäscher	Klatte
Frida Richard	Frau Heinicke

Director
Gerhard Lamprecht
Screenplay
Luise Heilborn-Körbitz
Gerhard Lamprecht
based on the works
of Heinrich Zille
Cinematography
Karl Hasselmann
Sets
Otto Moldenhauer
Production company
National-Film AG, Berlin
Premiere
28 August 1925, Berlin
Length
2,444 m, approx. 113 min.
Format
35 mm, b/w, silent

A prostitute named Emma (Aud Egede Nissen) takes pity on ex-con Kramer (Bernhard Goetzke).

Eduard Rothauser as Rottmann, an elderly photographer who offers Kramer the hope of a job.

1925

Varieté
Variety

After ten years in prison, the former circus performer 'Boss' Huller (Jannings) tells his life story, featuring a love triangle that ends with him stabbing his rival. 'A triumph of direction, photography and acting. In <u>Variety</u> there are scenes that set standards for the cinema in general, for the particular genre, and for its distinction from the drama of words. The aerial shots of the Winter Garden are superb. Equally superb are the contrasts between the fairground and the elegant variety show. Karl Freund's achievement is phenomenal' (Herbert Ihering, 1925).

Cast
Emil Jannings	'Boss' Huller
Lya de Putti	Berta-Marie
Warwick Ward	Artinelli
Maly Delschaft	Huller's wife
Georg John	Sailor
Kurt Gerron	Harbour worker
Charles Lincoln	Spanish artist
Alice Hechy	Actress
Georg Baselt	Agent
Rastelli	Juggler

Director
E. A. Dupont
Screenplay
E. A. Dupont
Cinematography
Karl Freund
Sets
O. F. Werndorff
Music
Ernö Rapée
Production company
Universum-Film AG (Ufa), Berlin
Producer
Erich Pommer
Premiere
16 November 1925, Berlin
Length
2,228 m, approx. 82 min.
Format
35 mm, b/w, silent

Warwick Ward, Lya de Putti and Emil Jannings are the central figures in a circus love triangle.

Above and below: Emil Jannings is Boss, an acrobat who leaves his wife for a circus girl, only to lose her to a rival performer.

Emil Jannings finds his happiness is short-lived.

Maly Delschaft as Boss Huller's wife, abandoned and left to care for their son.

1926

Tartüff
Tartuffe

Carl Mayer devised a subplot as a frame story for Molière's comedy, duplicating the legacy-hunting tale in a film within a film. The main plot is set in Prussia at the time of 'Old Fritz' (Frederick the Great). 'Film director Murnau's totally convincing and striking achievement derives from the fact that he sees the subject of hypocrisy and indoctrination in more general terms than simply theological. By translating such verbal action into one that is silent, the director has turned the spotlight on the very essence of hypocrisy: absolutely everything that can be expressed through the body with rolling, upward-gazing eyes, the lies, the helplessness, the horror, lechery articulated through teeth and lips, passion through the back....' (Luc Bondy, 2003).

Cast
Emil Jannings — Tartuffe
Werner Krauss — Orgon
Lil Dagover — Elmire
André Mattoni — Grandson
Lucie Höflich — Dorine
Rosa Valetti — Housekeeper
Hermann Picha — Old man

Director
F. W. Murnau
Screenplay
Carl Mayer
based on the play
by Molière
Cinematography
Karl Freund
Sets
Robert Herlth
Walter Röhrig
Costumes
Robert Herlth
Music
Giuseppe Becce
Production company
Universum-Film AG (Ufa),
Berlin
Producer
Erich Pommer
Premiere
25 January 1926, Berlin
Length
1,867 m, approx. 65 min.
Format
35 mm, b/w, silent

Werner Krauss as Orgon and Lil Dagover as Elmire.

Lil Dagover as Elmire and Emil Jannings as Tartuffe.

Die Brüder Schellenberg

The Brothers Schellenberg

A drama about two brothers whose personalities are totally different. Wenzel speculates successfully on the stock market and gets involved in numerous relationships; Michael wants to help humankind and sets up a shelter for the unemployed. When Wenzel believes he has been betrayed by his mistress, he kills her. Conrad Veidt plays both brothers. 'Grune focused more on one of these two very different brothers – on the adventurer, speculator and upstart Wenzel. He portrayed him as a typical figure of the twenties, diseased and ruined by the time. The stock exchange sequence especially captures the authentic background of the period. Against that background we experience the rise and fall of Wenzel Schellenberg. Grune pronounced moral judgment on his unscrupulous "hero" by making him go insane in the end' (Fred Gehler, 1988).

Cast

Conrad Veidt	Wenzel Schellenberg/ Michael Schellenberg
Lil Dagover	Esther Raucheisen
Liane Haid	Jenny Florian
Henry de Vries	Herr Raucheisen
Werner Fuetterer	Georg Weidenbach
Bruno Kastner	Kaczinsky
Julius Falkenstein	Esther's 1st suitor
Wilhelm Bendow	Esther's 2nd suitor
Erich Kaiser-Titz	Esther's 3rd suitor
Paul Morgan	Gangster
Frida Richard	Poor widow

Director
Karl Grune
Screenplay
Willy Haas
Karl Grune
based on the novel by
Bernhard Kellermann
Cinematography
Karl Hasselmann
Sets
Karl Görge
Kurt Kahle
Music
Werner Richard Heymann
Production
Universum-Film AG (Ufa),
Berlin
Producer
Erich Pommer
Premiere
23 March 1926, Berlin
Length
2,834 m, approx. 104 min.
Format
35 mm, b/w, silent

Conrad Veidt in his dual role as the brothers Schellenberg: the self-sacrificing Michael (left) and the ambitious Wenzel (right).

Lil Dagover as Esther Raucheisen, the heiress who becomes Wenzel Schellenberg's mistress.

Lil Dagover and Conrad Veidt at the film's tragic climax.

1926

Geheimnisse einer Seele

Secrets of a Soul

A case for Sigmund Freud. A chemistry professor's pathological fear of knives is cured by psychotherapy. Werner Krauss plays the patient. As the film had a documentary purpose, it was marketed by the Ufa Kulturfilm department. 'Psychoanalysis seeks to use clear images in order to straighten out people's mental confusion. This attempt to demonstrate its essence by means of a film is far from being the weird hocus-pocus that is the popular image so many people have. On the contrary, Secrets of a Soul is an extraordinarily clear-cut – and also very exciting – affair. The fact that this tale of psychiatric illness does not quite amount to a work of art, and that the harmony between scientific and artistic views of the soul does not lead to a creation of outstanding quality is the fault of the antediluvian rules of censorship in this Republic' (Axel Eggebrecht, 1926).

Cast

Werner Krauss	Martin Fellman
Ruth Weyher	The Wife
Ilka Grüning	The Mother
Jack Trevor	Erich
Pawel Pawlow	Doctor
Hertha von Walther	Assistant
Renate Brausewetter	Maid
Colin Ross	Chief of police

Director
G. W. Pabst
Screenplay
Colin Ross
Hans Neumann
Cinematography
Guido Seeber
Curt Oertel
Walter Robert Lach
Sets
Ernö Metzner
Production company
Neumann-Film-Produktion, Berlin
Producer
Hans Neumann
Premiere
24 March 1926, Berlin
Length
2,214 m, approx. 81 min.
Format
35 mm, b/w, silent

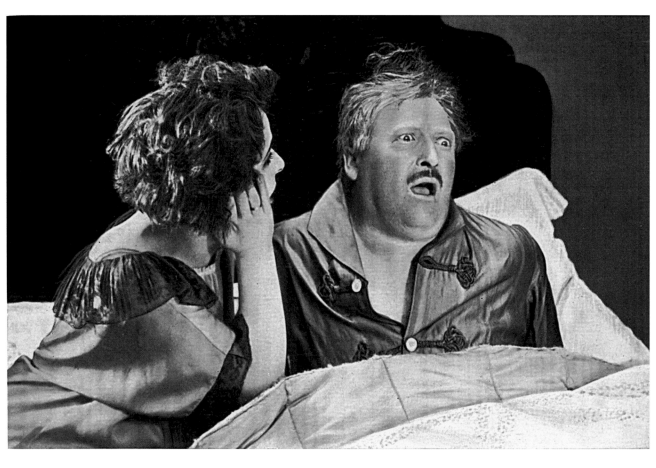

Martin Fellman (Werner Krauss) is tormented by his dreams, much to the distress of his wife (Ruth Weyher).

Camilla Horn as the innocent Gretchen.

Above: Mephisto (Emil Jannings) and Faust (Gösta Ekman) take flight.
Below: Mephisto's sword becomes the subject of some witty phallic symbolism.

Mephisto (Emil Jannings) creates a distraction by wooing Gretchen's Aunt Marthe (Yvette Guilbert).

Der heilige Berg
The Holy Mountain

A mountaineer and a skier fall in love with the same dancer. They quarrel during an expedition. There are falls, dramatic rescues, a snowstorm, and in the end both men fall to their deaths. 'Leni Riefenstahl introduced a new element into Arnold Fanck's Bergfilme – and into his life. That element was the self-confident woman, otherwise virtually invisible in his world.... Her characters assert themselves among the men – just as the actress herself did – and she casts her spell over two of them. The dancer Diotima in Der heilige Berg was the first such heroine. She was also the first of Riefenstahl's outsiders – marked out by their origins, status and vocation... The character's foreignness is related to her anti-realism, which is heavily emphasized' (Rainer Rother, 2000).

Cast

Leni Riefenstahl	Diotima
Luis Trenker	The Friend
Ernst Petersen	Vigo
Frida Richard	Mother
Friedrich Schneider	Colli
Hannes Schneider	Mountain guide

Director
Arnold Fanck
Screenplay
Arnold Fanck
Cinematography
Hans Schneeberger
Helmar Lerski
Sepp Allgeier
Sets
Leopold Blonder
Music
Edmund Meisel
Production company
Universum-Film AG (Ufa),
Berlin
Premiere
17 December 1926
Length
3,100 m, approx. 114 min.
Format
35 mm, b/w, silent

Diotima (Leni Riefenstahl) gazes out at the mountain landscape.

Leni Riefenstahl as Diotima, the dancer at the centre of the film's love triangle.

Above and opposite: The dying mountaineer dreams of being reunited with his beloved inside a cathedral of ice.

1927

Metropolis

A social drama about a city of the future. The rich and powerful live above, while the workers toil below in the dark to create their wealth. During a rebellion, led by a female robot, they destroy the means of production. But in the end there is reconciliation: the heart has to be the mediator between hand and brain. This is a vision that is as powerful as it is naïve. Technically it is a masterpiece, but it was not the worldwide success its makers had hoped for. Ufa reacted in the way that producers often do: they cut it, shortened it and mutilated it. When the film subsequently became a cinematic legend, its reconstruction was a Sisyphean task.

Cast
Brigitte Helm	Maria/Machine
Alfred Abel	Joh Fredersen
Gustav Fröhlich	Freder Fredersen
Rudolf Klein-Rogge	Rotwang the Inventor
Fritz Rasp	Thin Man
Theodor Loos	Josaphat/Joseph
Erwin Biswanger	No. 11811
Heinrich George	Groth, foreman of the Heart Machine
Olaf Storm	Jan
Hanns Leo Reich	Marinus
Heinrich Gotho	Master of Ceremonies
Margarete Lanner	Lady in car/Woman in Eternal Gardens
Georg John	Worker

Director
Fritz Lang
Screenplay
Thea von Harbou
based on her novel
Cinematography
Günther Rittau
Karl Freund
Stills photography
Horst von Harbou
Sets
Otto Hunte
Erich Kettelhut
Karl Vollnrecht
Costumes
Änne Willkomm
Music
Gottfried Huppertz
Production company
Universum-Film AG (Ufa), Berlin
Producer
Erich Pommer
Premiere
10 January 1927, Berlin
Length
4,189 m, approx. 153 min.
Format
35 mm, b/w, silent

The inventor Rotwang (Rudolf Klein-Rogge, right) shows his robot creation (Brigitte Helm) to Joh Fredersen (Alfred Abel, left).

Operated by an army of workers, the Heart Machine powers the city of Metropolis.

Metropolis

The towers of Metropolis are home to the wealthy,
while the workers live underground.

Above: Margarete Lanner and Gustav Fröhlich in an idyllic rooftop garden.
Below: The robot is given the human form of Maria (Brigitte Helm) to spread dissent among the workers.

Above: The idealistic Freder Fredersen (Gustav Fröhlich, right) is shocked by the callousness of his father (Alfred Abel).
Below: The false Maria (Brigitte Helm) performs in a nightclub in the city's red-light district.

Above: Joh Fredersen (Alfred Abel) speaks to one of his employees (Heinrich George) on a videophone.

Below: The real Maria (Brigitte Helm) struggles to operate a huge gong that will warn the workers of the rising flood waters.

Above: Freder (Gustav Fröhlich) helps a worker who has collapsed at his station by taking his place.
Below: Maria (Brigitte Helm) tries to save the children of the lower city.

Dirnentragödie
Tragedy of the Street

Drama set in the world of prostitution. It tells the tale of four people: the ageing prostitute Auguste, the young prostitute Clarissa, their pimp Anton and a student named Felix. Auguste does not find the happiness she longs for with Felix, Anton murders Clarissa and Auguste commits suicide. 'In their interplay, a minute extends to a huge span of time in which people are born, hope, suffer and die. A mimed monologue by Asta Nielsen is the most profound aesthetic pleasure to be found in the whole art of the cinema' (Willy Haas, 1927).

Cast

Asta Nielsen	Auguste
Hilde Jennings	Clarissa
Oskar Homolka	Anton
Werner Pittschau	Felix
Hedwig Pauly-Winterstein	Mother
Otto Kronburger	Father
Hermann Picha	Kauzke
Eva Speyer	Prostitute

Director
Bruno Rahn
Screenplay
Ruth Goetz
Leo Heller
based on the play
by Wilhelm Braun
Cinematography
Guido Seeber
Sets
Carl Ludwig Kirmse
Music
Felix Bartsch
Production company
Pantomim-Film AG, Berlin
Premiere
14 April 1927, Berlin
Length
2,388 m, approx. 80 min.
Format
35 mm, b/w, silent

Auguste (Asta Nielsen) hopes that Felix (Werner Pittschau) will be her key to a new life.

Auguste (Asta Nielsen) prepares herself for another night on the streets.

1927

Der Fürst von Pappenheim

The Masked Mannequin

A farce set in the world of fashion. Pappenheim is a flourishing fashion house in Berlin, whose leading salesman is named Egon Fürst. A runaway princess is secretly working there as a model. Her strait-laced uncle has a stately home in Baden-Baden, and this becomes the setting for a fashion show that provides a dazzling finale. Curt Bois enthusiastically explores all the comic possibilities of disguise, including cross-dressing. 'Into the midst of a social, "new objectivity" comedy, among stiff gentlemen and starched ladies – all apparently straight from the theatre of light entertainment – comes this absolute livewire. A little man bent on survival, with a temperament that might be called a mixture of Chaplin and Lloyd, but who has to switch identities quicker than the two of them put together' (Thomas Brandlmeier, 1985).

Cast

Curt Bois	Egon Fürst
Mona Maris	Princess Antoinette
Dina Gralla	Diana
Lydia Potechina	Camilla Pappenheim
Hans Junkermann	Prince Ottokar
Werner Fuetterer	Sascha, Prince of Gorgonia
Julius von Szöreghy	Count Katschkoff
Albert Paulig	Prince's adjutant

Director
Richard Eichberg
Screenplay
Robert Liebmann
based on the operetta
by Arnold and Bach
Cinematography
Heinrich Gärtner
Bruno Mondi
Sets
Jacques Rotmil
Music
Artur Guttmann
Giuseppe Becce
Production company
Eichberg-Film GmbH,
Berlin, for Ufa
Producer
Richard Eichberg
Premiere
7 September 1927, Berlin
Length
2,306 m, approx. 90 min.
Format
35 mm, b/w, silent

A salesman (Curt Bois) finds love with a model (Mona Maris) who is actually a runaway princess.

Role reversal: Curt Bois tries his hand at modelling, with Mona Maris as his dapper escort.

Curt Bois plays the hapless fashion salesman, surrounded by beautiful models.

Berlin. Die Sinfonie der Grossstadt
Berlin: Symphony of a Great City

Twenty-four hours in the life of Germany's capital city. Documentary footage is edited together like a musical composition. The focus is on creating a visual effect rather than reflecting social conditions, and in this respect it is an avant-garde piece of filmmaking. The original idea came from Carl Mayer, but he was not happy with the direction of the project and left the production team. 'According to what we have heard, the idea was to create an abstract, animated fantasy which – whether for better or for worse – would remain an interesting experiment, or perhaps a showpiece. However, what we then saw was something quite different. An utterly daring and undoubtedly epoch-making attempt to capture the very meat of reality' (Roland Schacht, 1927).

Director
Walther Ruttmann
Screenplay
Walther Ruttmann
Karl Freund
based on an idea
by Carl Mayer
Cinematography
Reimar Kuntze
Robert Baberske
László Schäffer
Karl Freund
(camera supervisor)
Editing
Walther Ruttmann
Music
Edmund Meisel
Production company
Fox-Europa, Berlin
Premiere
23 September 1927, Berlin
Length
1,466 m, approx. 62 min.
Format
35 mm, b/w, silent

Above and opposite: Instead of using conventional stills, the film was publicized with these specially commissioned photomontages.

Die Liebe der Jeanne Ney

The Love of Jeanne Ney / Lusts of the Flesh

The love affair between a French girl and a Russian revolutionary in the Crimea and in Paris is repeatedly thwarted by a blackmailer. The film stripped the source material of its political bite, and the author Ilja Ehrenburg protested in vain when his story was given a happy ending. 'The concept of épater le bourgeois is taken to extremes. Somewhere in Paris, a dirty little runt earns his living doing shady deals. The camera stalks him, and shows him in the most ridiculous poses, goggle-eyed, repulsively smacking his lips, and by unnaturally magnifying the perspective, it humiliates him. It mocks him, unmasks him, drills into his skull and lays bare the mediocre brain of the petit bourgeois. G.W. Pabst as the heir to the values of Expressionism' (Hans Feld, 1927).

Cast

Edith Jéhanne	Jeanne Ney
Brigitte Helm	Gabriele Ney
Hertha von Walther	Margot
Uno Henning	Andreas
Fritz Rasp	Khalibiev
Adolf Edgar Licho	Raymond Ney
Eugen Jensen	Alfred Ney
Hans Járay	Emile Poitras
Wladimir Sokoloff	Zacharkiewicz
Siegfried Arno	Gaston
Jack Trevor	Mr Jack

Director
G. W. Pabst
Screenplay
Ilja Ehrenburg
Ladislaus Vajda
Rudolf Leonhard
based on the book
by Ilja Ehrenburg
Cinematography
Fritz Arno Wagner
Walter Robert Lach
Sets
Otto Hunte
Victor Trivas
Music
Hans May
Production company
Universum-Film AG (Ufa),
Berlin
Premiere
6 December 1927, Berlin
Length
2,643 m, approx. 97 min.
Format
35 mm, b/w, silent

Fritz Rasp plays the sinister Khalibiev.

A dream sequence: Jeanne fears her beloved Andreas will be sent to the guillotine.

Jeanne (Edith Jéhanne, right) is brought before the Bolshevik leaders.

Doña Juana

A comedy of cross-dressing and mistaken identities. Doña Juana, daughter of an impoverished aristocrat, is in love with Don Ramón. But his father has already promised that his son will marry the daughter of a rich business partner. Juana has been brought up as a boy, and uses all the tricks of androgyny to achieve her goal. Finally, the two fathers give in. 'In Doña Juana, based on a comedy by Tirso de Molina, the director puts a comfortable end to the emancipatory rebellion. Men as tall and broad as a wardrobe stand in the way of delicate little women. But here any direct conflict is automatically avoided. As Doña Juana, Bergner escapes through the back door from her father – who sits like a tyrant on his throne – slips out of her female role into the guise of a boy, and for the time being is liberated from all her cares' (Sibylle Wirsing, 1983).

Cast

Elisabeth Bergner	Doña Juana
Walter Rilla	Don Ramón
Hertha von Walther	Ines
Hubert von Meyerinck	Don Alfonso
Wolfgang von Schwind	Servant
Max Schreck	Doña Juana's father
Lotte Stein	Juana's maid
Li Hayda	Friend

Director
Paul Czinner
Screenplay
Béla Balázs
Paul Czinner
based on the play
by Tirso de Molina
Cinematography
Karl Freund
Robert Baberske
Sets
Erich Kettelhut
Leo Pasetti
Costumes
Leo Pasetti
Edith Glück
Music
Giuseppe Becce
Production company
Poetic-Film GmbH,
Berlin, for Ufa
Producer
Paul Czinner
Premiere
24 January 1928, Berlin
Length
3,081 m, approx. 104 min.
Format
35 mm, b/w, silent

Elisabeth Bergner as Doña Juana, with Hertha von Walther as Ines.

Above: Doña Juana (Elisabeth Bergner) disguises herself as a gentleman, Don Gil.
Below: Juana confronts her stern father (Max Schreck).

Spione

Spies

Thriller. Bank manager Haghi leads a double life as a master spy, but government agent Donald Tremaine, with the aid of Haghi's female employee, sets out on his trail. 'This is an attempt to synthesize powerful, indeed the most powerful material with modern, indeed the most modern forms of expression. The synthesis works well, and with it Fritz Lang continues the traditions of his own unforgettable Mabuse and some of the great films of Joe May. Let us hope that this subject will herald a renaissance of the genuinely exciting thriller, made with truly artistic means, in the German film industry' (Hans Wollenberg, 1928).

Cast

Rudolf Klein-Rogge	Haghi
Gerda Maurus	Sonja Barranikowa
Willy Fritsch	Donald Tremaine, Agent 326
Lien Dyers	Kitty
Louis Ralph	Morrier
Craighall Sherry	Police Chief Miles Jason
Paul Hörbiger	Franz the chauffeur
Hertha von Walther	Lady Leslane
Lupu Pick	Dr Masimoto
Fritz Rasp	Colonel Jellusic
Julius Falkenstein	Hotel manager

Director
Fritz Lang
Screenplay
Thea von Harbou
Fritz Lang
based on the novel
by Thea von Harbou
Cinematography
Fritz Arno Wagner
Stills photography
Horst von Harbou
Sets
Otto Hunte
Karl Vollbrecht
Music
Werner Richard Heymann
Production company
Fritz Lang-Film, for Ufa
Producer
Fritz Lang
Premiere
22 March 1928, Berlin
Length
4,364 m, approx. 143 min.
Format
35 mm, b/w, silent

Rudolf Klein-Rogge as master spy Haghi, in disguise as a clown.

Left: Sonja (Gerda Maurus) is the seductive Russian assigned to trick Agent 326 but instead she falls in love with him.
Right: Agent 326 (Willy Fritsch) poses as a vagrant to infiltrate the spy ring.

1928

Zuflucht
Refuge

Cast
Henny Porten	Hanne Lorek
Franz Lederer	Martin
Max Maximilian	Schurich
Margarete Kupfer	Frau Schurich
Alice Hechy	Guste, their daughter
Carl de Vogt	Kölling
Mathilde Sussin	Frau Falkhagen
Bodo Bronsky	Otto Falkhagen
Lotte Stein	Marie Jankowsky
Rudolf Biebrach	Doctor

Director
Carl Froelich
Screenplay
Friedrich Raff
Cinematography
Gustave Preiss
Sets
Franz Schroedter
Music
Walter Winnig
Production company
Henny Porten-Froelich
Produktion, Berlin
Producers
Henny Porten
Carl Froelich
Premiere
3 August 1928, Berlin
Length
2,510 m, approx. 95 min.
Format
35 mm, b/w, silent

Social drama. The love story of Hanne, a market trader, and Martin, the revolutionary son of a factory owner, is overshadowed by unemployment and the housing shortage. The ailing Martin gets a job working on the construction of the U-Bahn, but collapses and dies, leaving a pregnant Hanne to be cared for by his mother. 'Partially shot in authentic surroundings, and otherwise in artistically lit scenes, the film shows Porten as a straightforward and sensitive market worker who becomes attached to an idealistic but failed Spartacist. (Porten herself discovered Franz Lederer, who was well cast as the vulnerable and melancholy Martin.) It probably works better today than it did when viewed from the contemporary critical perspective of the middle-class bourgeoisie contemplating the "ugly truth" of proletarian misery' (Corinna Müller, 1990).

Hanne (Henny Porten) and Martin (Franz Lederer) face an uncertain future.

Above: Henny Porten as Hanne (centre) in the market where she works, with Margarete Kupfer (right).
Below: Alice Hechy, Franz Lederer, Henny Porten and Rudolf Biebrach.

Heimkehr

Homecoming

Two German friends become prisoners of war in Siberia. They escape, but one of them is recaptured. When he finally comes home, it is only to learn that he has lost his wife to his friend. The film is based on the novella Karl and Anna by Leonhard Frank but the author did not like the film version. 'May paid no attention to the socially accurate portrayal of the working-class environment. He was interested in the psychology of a melodramatic love triangle, which he captured in a cinematically dense atmosphere that depended entirely on the body language of the actors and a few decorative and lighting effects. The fact that the working-class woman is not wearing faded overalls but a blouse that shows off her feminine curves, and that there is light playing round her hair and accentuating a shimmering eroticism, is in keeping with the narrative and visual requirements of the cinema audience' (Jürgen Kasten, 1990).

Cast
Lars Hanson   Richard
Dita Parlo   Anna
Gustav Fröhlich   Karl
Theodor Loos
Philipp Manning

Director
Joe May
Screenplay
Joe May
Fritz Wendhausen
based on a novella
by Leonhard Frank
Cinematography
Günther Rittau
Sets
Julius von Borsody
Music
Willy Schmidt-Gentner
Production company
Universum-Film AG (Ufa),
Berlin
Producer
Erich Pommer
Premiere
29 August 1928, Berlin
Length
3,006 m, approx. 110 min.
Format
35 mm, b/w, silent

Dita Parlo tries to resist the attraction of her husband's best friend.

Above: Stascha (Marlene Dietrich) and her older lover (Fritz Kortner) have conspired to murder her husband.
Below: Stascha's softer side is awoken by Henri (Uno Henning).

1929

Tagebuch einer Verlorenen
Diary of a Lost Girl

Pabst's second film with Louise Brooks. She plays Thymian, an apothecary's daughter, who is raped by her father's assistant and ends up in a reformatory for wayward girls. Many of the scenes take place in a brothel, which made the film a prime target for the censors. 'The house of pleasure, with the happy and good-natured madam played by Vera Pawlowa, and the cheerful and pretty cocotte played by the strikingly gifted Edith Meinhard, creates a gentle, soft and seductive impression that offers a better world and indeed the only world still open after those first profound shocks of real life. And Louise Brooks makes her way through the film in silent beauty, frightened, stubborn, waiting, wondering, as the girl to whom things simply happen. She is almost like a beautiful, tragic Buster Keaton, wide-eyed, childlike, and enchantingly dressed' (Ernst Blass, 1929).

Cast

Louise Brooks	Thymian Henning
Fritz Rasp	Meinert
Edith Meinhard	Erika
Vera Pawlowa	Aunt Frieda
Josef Rovensky	Henning the apothecary
André Roanne	Count Nicolas Osdorff
Arnold Korff	Elder Count Osdorff
Andrews Engelmann	Director of the reformatory
Valeska Gert	Director's wife
Siegfried Arno	Guest
Kurt Gerron	Dr Vitalis

Director
G. W. Pabst
Screenplay
Rudolf Leonhard
based on the novel by
Margarethe Boehme
Cinematography
Sepp Allgeier
Sets
Ernö Metzner
Emil Hasler
Music
Otto Stenzel
Production company
Pabst-Film GmbH, Berlin
Producer
G. W. Pabst
Premiere
27 September 1929, Vienna
Length
2,863 m, approx. 116 min.
Format
35 mm, b/w, silent

Louise Brooks as Thymian.

On the day of her confirmation, Thymian (Louise Brooks) is left alone in her father's shop with his assistant Meinert (Fritz Rasp).

Meinert rapes his employer's daughter Thymian and leaves her pregnant.

Thymian ends up in a high-class brothel, where Dr Vitalis (Kurt Gerron) is a client.

Die weisse Hölle vom Piz Palü

The White Hell of Pitz Palu

A couple join a lone mountaineer on an expedition to climb Pitz Palu in the Italian Alps. The loner falls victim to the mountain that killed his wife, but the couple are rescued. This film of ice and snow was hugely successful. 'The camera pans over a landscape that is visually defined, shaped and varied like a woman. In this sense, mountains, like women, are projections of a certain fear, a desire for form, and an instrumental jealousy – they are something that attracts and yet frightens men, fascinating their eyes but threatening their lives – elemental forces that are available and that men strive to control and to keep in their power' (Erich Rentschler, 1989).

Cast

Gustav Diessl	Dr Johannes Krafft
Leni Riefenstahl	Maria Majoni
Ernst Petersen	Hans Brandt
Ernst Udet	Flier
Mizzi Götzel	Maria Krafft
Otto Spring	Christian Klucker
Kurt Gerron	Man in nightclub

Directors
Arnold Fanck
G. W. Pabst
Screenplay
Arnold Fanck
Ladislaus Vajda
Cinematography
Sepp Allgeier
Richard Angst
Hans Schneeberger
Stills photography
Hans G. Casparius
Sets
Ernö Metzner
Music
Willy Schmidt-Gentner
Production company
H.R. Sokal-Film GmbH, Berlin
Producer
Henry Sokal
Premiere
11 October 1929, Vienna
Length
3,330 m, approx. 113 min.
Format
35 mm, b/w, silent

Trapped on a high ledge, Maria (Leni Riefenstahl) tries to wake Krafft (Gustav Diessl).

The beauty and danger of the mountains is captured by the striking cinematography.

Frau im Mond

Woman in the Moon / By Rocket to the Moon

A combination of science fiction and a melodramatic love story. A rocket goes to the moon, carrying six people (including a blind passenger). Once they are there, a fatal quarrel ensues over the gold that they find. Only two of them return to Earth. Fritz Lang's technical advisers were Hermann Oberth and Willy Ley, two bona fide rocket experts. The moonscape was constructed in the Neubabelsberg studio. The director was later very proud of his invention of the countdown for the intertitles of this silent film: 'When I shot the take-off, I said, "If I count one, two, three, four, ten, fifty, hundred – an audience doesn't know when it will go off. But if I count down – ten, nine, eight, seven, six, five, four, three, two, one, ZERO! – then they will know"' (1967).

Cast

Gerda Maurus	Friede Velten
Willy Fritsch	Wolf Helius
Klaus Pohl	Professor Georg Manfeldt
Gustav von Wangenheim	Hans Windegger
Gustl Stark-Gstettenbaur	Gustav
Fritz Rasp	Walt Turner
Tilla Durrieux	Brain with a chequebook
Hermann Vallentin	Brain with a chequebook
Max Zilzer	Brain with a chequebook
Mahmud Terja Bey	Brain with a chequebook
Borwin Walth	Brain with a chequebook

Director
Fritz Lang
Screenplay
Thea von Harbou
based on her novel
Cinematography
Curt Courant
Otto Kanturek
Stills photography
Horst von Harbou
Sets
Otto Hunte
Emil Hasler
Karl Vollbrecht
Music
Willy Schmidt-Gentner
Production company
Universum-Film AG (Ufa),
Berlin
Producer
Fritz Lang
Premiere
15 October 1929, Berlin
Length
4,365 m, approx. 169 min.
Format
35 mm, b/w, silent

Hans Windegger (Gustav von Wangenheim) is the mission's chief engineer, while the industrialist Helius (Willy Fritsch) is its driving force.

Above: Friede (Gerda Maurus) has no need for a helmet because the far side of the moon has a breathable atmosphere.
Below: Helius (Willy Fritsch, right) walks out of the rocket with stowaway Gustav (Gustl Stark-Gstettenbaur).

1929

Karl Valentin, der Sonderling
The Odd Man

The only full-length silent film to feature the hugely popular Bavarian comedian Karl Valentin. His famous wordplay is confined to the intertitles. He plays a journeyman tailor who becomes the target of his boss's wife's romantic interest, while he himself is more interested in postage stamps. When he discovers a particularly rare one in his album, he is unjustly arrested for theft. On his release from prison, he makes several unsuccessful attempts to kill himself, but refuses to go on a motorcycle ride with the boss's infatuated wife, claiming 'I'm not yet tired of life.' 'A rich plot full of surprises and basic comic situations. Well acted and well photographed. And so one leaves the theatre in the best of moods. It is of course only later, when the hilarity has subsided, that we become fully conscious of the artistry of this great comedian' (Wilhelm Lucas Kristl, 1929).

Cast
Karl Valentin — Tailor
Liesl Karlstadt — Paula Kuhn
Truus von Aalten — Anni, her niece
Ferdinand Martini — Friedrich Kuhn, master tailor
Heinz Koennecke — Herr Lechner, Anni's suitor
Gustl Stark-Gstettenbaur — Toni, clockmaker's apprentice

Director
Walter Jerven
Screenplay
Walter Jerven
Cinematography
Hans Karl Gottschalk
Sets
Peter Rochelsberg
Music
Trauter
Production company
Union-Film-Co. GmbH, Munich
Producers
Franz Osten
Walter Jerven
Premiere
28 December 1929, Munich
Length
2,508 m, approx. 88 min.
Format
35 mm, b/w, silent

Karl Valentin attracts the unwelcome attentions of his boss's wife (Liesl Karlstadt).

Above and below: Karl Valentin's attempts to find a rare stamp lead to mishaps and misunderstandings.

Above and opposite: Karl Valentin was an enormously popular star of his era, combining physical clowning with a satirical edge.

Mutter Krausens Fahrt ins Glück

Mother Krause's Journey to Happiness

Based on accounts by Heinrich Zille, in which he denounced the appalling living conditions of people in the working-class districts of Berlin. Mother Krause, who delivers newspapers for a living, kills herself after her son, Paul, misappropriates the subscription money. A naturalistic melodrama made by the Communist production company Prometheus Film. 'Here we have one of the artistically most direct, histrionically most realistic, and conceptually most honest German films, directed and shot by the Russian Phil Jutzi. He is a supreme master of the techniques of the Russian cinema. However, he does not use them for virtuoso effects, but in every brilliant cut and fade, in every focus on a particular detail as the dominant image, he clearly brings out the purpose and meaning, so that the symbolic value of the image is always given concrete form' (Fritz Walter, 1930).

Cast

Alexandra Schmitt	Mother Krause
Holmes Zimmermann	Paul Krause, her son
Ilse Trautschold	Erna Krause, her daughter
Gerhard Bienert	Lodger
Vera Sacharowa	Friede, a prostitute
Fee Wachsmuth	Friede's daughter
Friedrich Gnass	Max, a workman

Director
Phil Jutzi
Screenplay
Willy Döll
Jan Fethke
based on the stories
of Heinrich Zille
Cinematography
Phil Jutzi
Sets
Robert Scharfenberg
Carl Haacker
Music
Paul Dessau
Production company
Prometheus Film-Verleih
und Vertrieb, Berlin
Producer
Willi Münzenberg
Premiere
30 December 1929, Berlin
Length
3,297 m, approx. 120 min.
Format
35 mm, b/w, silent

A meagre meal in Mother Krause's apartment. From left to right: Vera Sacharowa (standing), Fee Wachsmuth, Alexandra Schmitt as Mother Krause, Friedrich Gnass, Ilse Trautschold, Gerhard Bienert.

Mother Krause's lodger (Gerhard Bienert) turns a lustful eye on her daughter Erna (Ilse Trautschold).

1930

Menschen am Sonntag
People on Sunday

Five young people go for a weekend break in Berlin: a wine dealer, a film extra, a sales assistant in a record shop, a taxi driver and his model girlfriend. Saturday is spent in the city, and Sunday out in the country. Five young filmmakers made a documentary of it, using amateur actors in a silent, pointillist film study. Only Eugen Schüfftan the cameraman was a professional. 'It is always amazing how much they knew at that time about camerawork and what beautiful pictures they made. They had a sense for detail and for what could be done with clever editing. I find it extremely impressive. Of course the charm of the film lies in the fact that it is so carefree, and that it takes the simplicity of this Sunday afternoon as its subject matter. The fact that it says: this is a tale worth telling' (Wolfgang Kohlhaase, 2008).

Cast
Erwin Splettstösser — Erwin, taxi driver
Brigitte Borchert — Brigitte, record shop sales assistant
Wolfgang von Waltershausen — Wolfgang, wine dealer
Christl Ehlers — Christl, film extra
Annie Schreyer — Annie, model
Kurt Gerron — Passer-by
Valeska Gert — Passer-by

Directors
Robert Siodmak
Edgar G. Ulmer
Screenplay
Billie Wilder
based on an article by Kurt Siodmak
Cinematography
Eugen Schüfftan
Camera assistant
Fred Zinnemann
Music
Otto Stenzel
Production company
Filmstudio 1929, Berlin
Producers
Moritz Seeler
Heinrich Nebenzahl
Premiere
4 February 1930, Berlin
Length
2,014 m, approx. 73 min.
Format
35 mm, b/w, silent

The film used amateur actors in real-life settings to achieve a new kind of cinematic naturalism.

From left to right: Erwin Splettstösser, Christl Ehlers, Brigitte Borchert and Wolfgang von Waltershausen.

Der Blaue Engel
The Blue Angel

Rath, a petit bourgeois high-school teacher, falls for Lola Lola, an opportunistic singer at the Blue Angel nightclub. After their marriage, he humiliates himself playing a clown for the troupe, and finally loses his mind during a performance in his hometown. The posters advertised this as an 'Emil Jannings film', but Marlene Dietrich was the true star of the show. 'Lola Lola's vitality and her open display of sexuality provide the solid base for her clear-cut character, which follows the rules of a barter society. Rath's world, on the other hand, is governed by a merely superficial and fundamentally rotten morality. Lola Lola wrecks this world of hypocrisy and second-hand wisdom. Immanuel Rath and Lola Lola are not simply prototypes of their respective sexes, but far more: they represent modernity and conservatism' (Werner Sudendorf, 2001).

Cast

Emil Jannings	Professor Immanuel Rath
Marlene Dietrich	Lola Lola
Kurt Gerron	Kiepert
Rosa Valetti	Guste Kiepert
Hans Albers	Mazeppa
Reinhold Bernt	Clown
Eduard von Winterstein	Headmaster
Johannes Roth	Pedell

Director
Josef von Sternberg
Screenplay
Robert Liebmann
Karl Vollmöller
based on the novel
by Heinrich Mann
Cinematography
Günther Rittau
Sets
Otto Hunte
Emil Hasler
Costumes
Tihamér Varady
Music
Friedrich Hollaender
Production company
Universum-Film AG (Ufa),
Berlin
Producer
Erich Pommer
Premiere
1 April 1930, Berlin
Length
2,965 m, 108 min.
Format
35 mm, b/w, sound

Professor Rath (Emil Jannings) visits the Blue Angel cabaret and becomes enraptured by its star, Lola Lola (Marlene Dietrich).

Marlene Dietrich as the seductive Lola Lola.

Marlene Dietrich became indelibly associated with the song
'Falling in Love Again'. Here she sings it for the first time.

Poverty stricken and humiliated, Rath (Emil Jannings, left) is obliged to work as a clown
and watch his wife Lola Lola (Marlene Dietrich) flirt with the strongman Mazeppa (Hans Albers).

Above left: Mack the Knife (Rudolf Forster) and Polly (Carola Neher) are married by a vicar (Hermann Thimig).   Above right: Mack pays a visit to the brothel.
Below left: Reinhold Schünzel and Rudolf Forster.   Below right: Lotte Lenya as Jenny and Wladimir Sokoloff as Smith.

249

1931

M

Lang's first talkie, with Lorre as the pathological child-murderer. The state authorities and the world of organized crime join forces to hunt him down. Concerning the M symbol, Wim Wenders said: 'It's an incredible, purely visual device, [the beggar] chalking the M on the palm of his hand and then pretending to stumble and transferring it onto the [murderer's] back. And this leads to what is really the greatest shot in the whole film, when Lorre stands in front of the mirror and discovers the M. In fact it encapsulates the whole film. Sometimes that happens – a single image tells the whole story. I don't know if anything similar has ever been done again in the cinema' (2008).

Cast

Peter Lorre	Hans Beckert
Ellen Widmann	Frau Beckmann
Inge Landgut	Elsie Beckmann
Gustaf Gründgens	Safe-cracker
Friedrich Gnass	Burglar
Fritz Odemar	Cheat
Paul Kemp	Pickpocket
Theo Lingen	Conman
Ernst Stahl-Nachbaur	Police chief
Franz Stein	Minister
Otto Wernicke	Inspector Lohmann
Theodor Loos	Inspector Groeber
Georg John	Blind panhandler

Director
Fritz Lang
Screenplay
Thea von Harbou
Fritz Lang
Cinematography
Fritz Arno Wagner
Robert Baberske
Stills photography
Horst von Harbou
Sets
Emil Hasler
Karl Vollbrecht
Music
Motif from Peer Gynt
by Edvard Grieg
Production company
Nero-Film AG, Berlin
Producer
Seymour Nebenzahl
Premiere
11 May 1931, Berlin
Length
3,208 m, 117 min.
Format
35 mm, b/w, sound

Peter Lorre as child-murderer Hans Beckert.

Inge Landgut as Elsie Beckmann: in the shadow of a killer.

Above: Elsie (Inge Landgut) looks into a toyshop window, under the gaze of Beckert (Peter Lorre).
Below: Beckert buys his victim a gift from a blind balloon seller (Georg John).

In a shop window, Beckert sees that he has been marked with an M for 'murderer'.

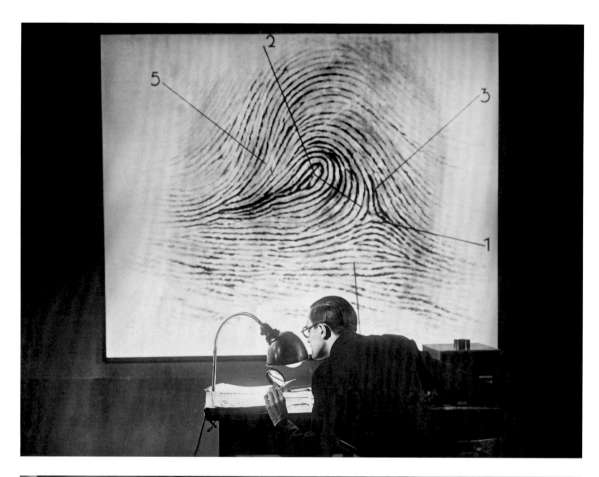

Above and below: Beckert is hunted by not one but two organizations.
The first is the police, with their advanced detection methods such as fingerprinting.

Above and below: Theo Lingen (above left), Friedrich Gnass, Gustaf Gründgens (above, second from right), Fritz Odemar and Paul Kemp (back to camera) are the second group of men on Beckert's trail: all members of the criminal underworld.

Beckert is tried before a kangaroo court, made up of criminals and other members of the city underworld.

Der Kongress tanzt

Congress Dances

The tale of a brief love affair between a glovemaker and the Russian Tsar, against the background of the Vienna Congress, is told as a lavish musical comedy. 'Charell as director has given the camera a free rein. It doesn't stand still for a second, and the scenes seem almost to be too short. The Heurige sung by the famous singer Paul Hörbiger is itself a cabaret act, a veritable showstopper, an encapsulation of everything Viennese that has ever been filmed. Everything is in motion, everything is in a whirl. The fades and cuts are superb, the sets and costumes magnificent, and musically the rhythms of sound and picture are perfectly in harmony. The Heurige dance blending into a ballet, and the empty congress seats swinging to the beat – these are dazzling effects created by Heymann. One is sometimes reminded of Lubitsch' (Pem, 1931).

Cast

Lilian Harvey	Christel Weinzinger
Willy Fritsch	Tsar Alexander of Russia
Otto Walburg	Bibikoff
Conrad Veidt	Prince Metternich
Carl-Heinz-Schroth	Pepi, Metternich's secretary
Lil Dagover	Countess
Alfred Abel	King of Saxony
Adele Sandrock	Princess
Margarete Kupfer	Countess
Julius Falkenstein	Finance minister
Ernst Stahl-Nachbaur	Napoleon
Paul Hörbiger	Singer

Director
Erik Charell
Screenplay
Norbert Falk
Robert Liebmann
Cinematography
Carl Hoffmann
Stills photography
Horst von Harbou
Sets
Robert Herlth
Walter Röhrig
Costumes
Ernst Stern
Music
Werner Richard Heymann
Production company
Universum-Film AG (Ufa),
Berlin
Producer
Erich Pommer
Premiere
29 September 1931, Vienna
Length
2,764 m, 101 min.
Format
35 mm, b/w, sound

Willy Fritsch and Lilian Harvey play the unlikely lovers who meet across the class divide.

Above: Lilian Harvey and Willy Fritsch take to the dancefloor.
Below: No expense was spared with the sumptuous sets.

Berlin-Alexanderplatz

A melodrama set in the underworld of Berlin, in which a small-time ex-convict, Franz Biberkopf, who is basically an honest man, strives to keep his head above water. Jutzi reduces the scale of Alfred Döblin's original novel. Fifty years later, Rainer Werner Fassbinder adapted the same book into an epic thirteen-part TV series. 'In the film, the life of suffering that marks the novel ends on the winner's podium. There he stands, the bold city adventurer, whom the audience is meant to see as a model man, whose iron will never falters even in the most difficult of situations, and indeed who actually needs these situations in order to show what a winner he is. A key element here is the way the film repeatedly incorporates Alexanderplatz. Because in contrast to the novel... it is in Alexanderplatz that Jutzi's Biberkopf increasingly demonstrates his strength in the face of events going on elsewhere in the city' (Guntram Voigt, 2001).

Cast

Heinrich George	Franz Biberkopf
Maria Bard	Cilly
Margarete Schlegel	Mieze
Bernhard Minetti	Reinhold
Gerhard Bienert	Klempner-Karl
Albert Florath	Pums
Paul Westermeier	Henschke

Director
Phil Jutzi
Screenplay
Alfred Döblin
Hans Wilhelm
based on the novel
by Alfred Döblin
Cinematography
Nikolaus Farkas
Stills photography
Fritz Vopel
Sets
Julius von Borsody
Costumes
Richard Timm
Alma Timm
Music
Allan Gray
Production company
Allianz-Tonfilm GmbH,
Berlin
Producer
Arnold Pressburger
Premiere
8 October 1931, Berlin
Length
2,395 m, 88 min.
Format
35 mm, b/w, sound

Franz Biberkopf (Heinrich George, centre) is teased by bar patrons for being a street trader.

Above: Biberkopf (Heinrich George) is caught between the desire to stay on the right side of the law and the temptations of crime.
Below: Biberkopf tries selling necktie holders to the crowds on Alexanderplatz.

1931

Mädchen in Uniform

The subtle romantic relationship between a female teacher and a schoolgirl in a boarding school leads to a conflict that has to be resolved in true Prussian style. With its all-female cast, this was one of the great international successes for German cinema. 'Hertha Thiele's Manuela has none of the clumsy awkwardness of a teenage girl. She is a seraphic being, with a slender body, upright posture, though her shoulders are always pushed slightly forwards. The ever anxious face is framed by the transparent blonde of her hair, with a full mouth that has a still indeterminate sensuality. Her voice is boyish, and one feels that at any moment it might break. The hint of something meltingly ethereal is countered by the materiality of her body. Hertha Thiele acts out every aspect of this ambivalence – a true artist of the transitory' (Karola Gramann/Heide Schlüpmann, 1983).

Cast
Hertha Thiele — Manuela von Meinhardis
Gertrud de Lalsky — Manuela's aunt
Dorothea Wieck — Fräulein von Bernburg
Emilie Unda — Fräulein von Nordeck zur Nidden, headmistress
Marte Hein — School governor
Hedwig Schlichter — Fräulein von Kesten
Erika Mann — Fräulein von Atems
Ellen Schwanneke — Ilse von Westhagen
Else Ehser — Else, wardrobe mistress
Ethel Reschke — Oda von Oldersleben

Director
Leontine Sagan
Screenplay
Christa Winsloe
F. D. Adam
based on a play
by Christa Winsloe
Cinematography
Reimar Kuntze
Franz Weihmayr
Stills photography
Eugen Klagemann
Walter Lichtenstein
Sets
Fritz Maurischat
Music
Hansom Milde-Meissner
Production company
Deutsche Film-
Gemeinschaft GmbH,
Berlin
Producer
Friedrich Pflughaupt
Premiere
27 November 1931, Berlin
Length
2,480 m, 91 min.
Format
35 mm, b/w, sound

The teachers and pupils assemble.

Fräulein von Bernburg (Dorothea Wieck) and Manuela (Hertha Thiele) come to share a forbidden bond.

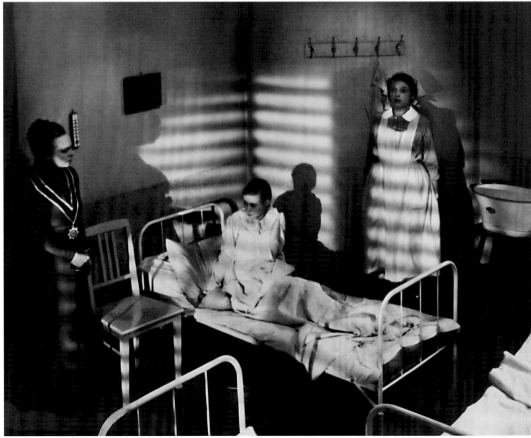

Above: The loneliness of new girl Manuela (Hertha Thiele) drives her to seek the kindness of Fräulein von Bernburg (Dorothea Wieck).
Below: Although treated kindly by Hanni (Miriam Lehmann-Haupt, right), Manuela attracts the fury of the headmistress (Emilie Unda, left).

Manuela (Hertha Thiele), in costume for a role in the school play, with her friend Ilse (Ellen Schwanneke, right).

1931

Emil und die Detektive
Emil and the Detectives

The classic tale of twelve-year-old Emil Tischbein, who has 120 marks stolen from him on the train from Neustadt to Berlin. Together with a lively gang of local boys and girls, he hunts down the thief (Fritz Rasp), who is already wanted by the police. 'A film about Berlin. Unobtrusively the city becomes not only the setting, but truly the one and only possible setting for this tale (in complete contrast to Emil's cosy little hometown), and as both Emil and the audience are taken on a journey of discovery through the big city, the film makes Berlin into an active participant in the plot' (Heinz-Gerd Rasner and Reinhard Wulf, 1980).

Cast

Käte Haack	Frau Tischbein
Rolf Wenkhaus	Emil Tischbein
Fritz Rasp	Grundeis
Rudolf Biebrach	Officer Jeschke
Olga Engl	Emil's grandmother
Inge Landgut	Pony Hütchen
Hans Joachim Schaufuss	Gustav
Hubert Schmitz	'The Professor'
Hans Richter	'Flying Stag'
Hans Albrecht Löhr	'Tuesday'

Director
Gerhard Lamprecht
Screenplay
Billie Wilder
based on the novel
by Erich Kästner
Cinematography
Werner Brandes
Stills photography
Emanuel Loewenthal
Sets
Werner Schlichting
Music
Allan Gray
Production company
Universum-Film AG
(Ufa), Berlin
Producer
Günther Stapenhorst
Premiere
2 December 1931, Berlin
Length
1,967 m, 72 min.
Format
35 mm, b/w, sound

Fritz Rasp as Grundeis, the villain of the piece.

Above: Hans Joachim Schaufuss as Gustav and Rolf Wenkhaus as Emil.
Below: Inge Landgut as Pony Hütchen.

Fritz Rasp as the shady Grundeis is followed by the gang of 'Detectives'.

Above: Fritz (Wolfgang Liebeneiner), Mizzi (Luise Ullrich) and Theo (Willy Eichberger).
Below: Two contrasting couples: Willy Eichberger and Luise Ullrich, with Magda Schneider and Wolfgang Liebeneiner.

Liebelei

Christine (Magda Schneider) and Mizzi (Luise Ullrich) look out for their sweethearts.

Portraits

The Stars of Weimar Cinema

Alfred Abel (1879–1937)
Photo: Atelier Binder

Hans Albers (1891–1960)

Albert Bassermann (1867–1952)

Curt Bois (1901–91)

Betty Amann (1905–90)

Fern Andra (1894–1974)

Anita Berber (1899–1928)

Elisabeth Bergner (1897–1986)
Photo: Hans G. Casparius

Ernst Busch (1900–80)

Ernst Deutsch (1890–1969)
Photo: Mac Walten

Gustav Diessl (1899–1948)

Wilhelm Dieterle (1893–1972)

Louise Brooks (1906–85)
Photo: Hans G. Casparius

Mady Christians (1900–51)

Lil Dagover (1887–1980)

Maly Delschaft (1898–1951)

Rudolf Forster (1884–1968)

Willy Fritsch (1901–73)
Photo: Atelier Binder

Gustav Fröhlich (1902–87)

Otto Gebühr (1877–1954)

Asta Nielsen (1881–1972)

Aud Egede Nissen (1893–1974)

Ossi Oswalda (1897–1947)

Dita Parlo (1907–71)

Fritz Rasp (1891–1976)

Paul Richter (1887–1961)

Max Schreck (1879–1936)
Photo: Lotte Jacobi

Reinhold Schünzel (1888–1954)

Henny Porten (1890–1960)

Lya de Putti (1897–1931)

Leni Riefenstahl (1902–2003)

Hertha Thiele (1908–84)

Karl Valentin (1882–1948)

Conrad Veidt (1893–1943)

Gustav von Wangenheim (1895–1975)

Paul Wegener (1874–1948)

Olga Tschechowa (1887–1980)

Hertha von Walther (1903–87)

Gertrud Welcker (1896–1988)

Ruth Weyher (1901–83)

Bibliography and Sources

Historical Overviews

Ursula Büttner, *Weimar. Die überforderte Republik. Leistung und Versagen in Staat, Gesellschaft, Wirtschaft und Kultur*, Stuttgart: Klett-Cotta, 2008

Anton Kaes, Martin Jay and Edward Dimendberg (eds.), *The Weimar Republic Sourcebook*, Berkeley, CA, and London: University of California Press, 1994; with 327 contemporary texts

Eberhard Kolb, *Die Weimarer Republik*, Munich: Oldenbourg, 2009; 7th revised ed.

Detlef Lehnert, *Die Weimarer Republik. Parteienstaat und Massengesellschaft*, Stuttgart: Reclam, 2009; 2nd ed.

Horst Möller, *Die Weimarer Republik. Eine unvollendete Demokratie*, Munich: dtv, 2004; 7th ed.

Ernst Nolte, *Die Weimarer Republik. Demokratie zwischen Lenin und Hitler*, Munich: Herbig, 2006

Manfred Overesch and Friedrich Wilhelm Saal, *Die Weimarer Republik. Eine Tageschronik der Politik, Wirtschaft, Kultur*, Düsseldorf: Droste, 1982

Heinrich August Winkler, *Weimar 1918–1933. Die Geschichte der ersten deutschen Demokratie*, Munich: Beck, 1998; revised ed.

Weimar Art, Culture and Society

Katharina von Ankum (ed.), *Women in the Metropolis: Gender and Modernity in Weimar Culture*, Berkeley, CA: University of California Press, 1997

Ralf Beil and Claudia Dillmann (eds.), *The Total Artwork in Expressionism: Art, Film, Literature, Theater, Dance, and Architecture, 1905–25*, Ostfildern: Hatje Cantz, 2010

Bernard von Brentano, *Wo in Europa ist Berlin? Bilder aus den zwanziger Jahren*, Frankfurt am Main: Insel, 1981

Kathleen Canning, Kerstin Barndt and Kristin McGuire (eds.), *Weimar Publics/Weimar Subjects: Rethinking the Political Culture of Germany in the 1920s*, Oxford: Berghahn, 2010

Julia Freytag and Alexandra Tacke (eds.), *City Girls. Bubiköpfe & Blaustrümpfe in den 1920er Jahren*, Cologne: Böhlau, 2011

Fritz Giese, *Girlkultur. Vergleiche zwischen amerikanischem und europäischem Rhythmus und Lebensgefühl*, Munich: Delphin-Verlag, 1925

Jost Hermand and Frank Trommler, *Kultur der Weimarer Republik*, Munich: Nymphenburger, 1978

Anton Kaes (ed.), *Kino-Debatte. Texte zum Verhältnis von Literatur und Film 1909–1929*, Tübingen: Max Niemeyer; Munich: dtv, 1978

Anton Kaes (ed.), *Weimarer Republik. Manifeste und Dokumente zur deutschen Literatur 1918–1933*, Stuttgart: Metzler, 1983

Christoph Kleinschmidt, *Intermaterialität. Zum Verhältnis von Schrift, Bild, Film und Bühne im Expressionismus*, Bielefeld: Transcript, 2012

Anita Kühnel (ed.), *Verführungen. Plakate aus Österreich und Deutschland von 1914 bis 1945*, Heidelberg: Umschau Braus, 1998

Gilles Neret, *The Arts of the Twenties: Painting, Sculpture, Architecture, Design, Theater Design, Graphic Art, Photography, Film*, New York: Rizzoli, 1986

Peter de Mendelssohn, *Zeitungsstadt Berlin. Menschen und Mächte in der Geschichte der deutschen Presse*, Berlin: Ullstein, 1959 and 1982

Rainer Metzger, *Berlin in the Twenties: Art and Culture 1918–1933*, London: Thames & Hudson, 2007

Hans Puttnies, *Das Gesicht der Weimarer Republik. Menschenbild und Bildkultur 1918–1933*, Berlin: Deutsches Historisches Museum, 2000

Günther Rühle, *Theater für die Republik*, Frankfurt am Main: S. Fischer, 1967, 1989, 2 vols.

Claudia Schmölders and Sander Gilman (eds.), *Gesichter der Weimarer Republik. Eine physiognomische Kulturgeschichte*, Cologne: DuMont, 2000

Christiane Schönfeld (ed.), *Practicing Modernity: Female Creativity in the Weimar Republic*, Würzburg: Königshausen & Neumann, 2006

Kristine von Soden and Maruta Schmidt (eds.), *Neue Frauen. Die zwanziger Jahre*, Berlin: Elefanten Press, 1988

John Alexander Williams (ed.), *Weimar Culture Revisited*, Basingstoke: Palgrave Macmillan, 2011

Weimar Film

1. Contemporary Publications

Curt Andersen, *Die deutsche Filmindustrie*, Munich: C.I.C. Andersen, 1929

Rudolf Arnheim, *Film als Kunst*, Berlin: Ernst Rowohlt, 1932; English ed.: *Film as Art*, London: Faber, 1969

Guido Bagier, *Der kommende Film*, Stuttgart, Berlin and Leipzig: Deutsche Verlags-Anstalt, 1928

Béla Balázs, *Der sichtbare Mensch*, Vienna and Leipzig: Deutsch-Österreichischer Verlag, 1924

Béla Balázs, *Der Geist des Films*, Halle: Wilhelm Knapp, 1930; English ed.: *Early Film Theory: Visible Man and The Spirit of Film*, trans. Rodney Livingstone, ed. Erica Carter, Oxford and New York: Berghahn Books, 2010

Edgar Beyfuss and A. Kossowsky (eds.), *Das Kulturfilmbuch*, Berlin: C. P. Chryselius'scher Verlag, 1924

Walter Bloem, *Seele des Lichtspiels*, Leipzig and Zurich: Grethlein & Co., 1922

Max Brod and Rudolf Thomas, *Liebe im Film*, Giessen: Kindt & Bucher, 1930

Edmund Bucher and Albrecht Kindt (eds.), *Film-Photos wie noch nie*, Giessen: Kindt & Bucher, 1929

Hans Buchner, *Im Banne des Films: Die Weltherrschaft des Kinos*, Munich: Deutscher Volksverlag, 1927

Oskar Diehl, *Mimik im Film*, Munich: Georg Müller, 1922

Ewald André Dupont, *Wie ein Film geschrieben wird und wie man ihn verwertet*, Berlin: Reinhold Kühn, 1919

Hans Erdmann and Giuseppe Becce, *Allgemeines Handbuch der Film-Musik*, Berlin: Schlesinger'sche Buch- und Musikhandlung, 1917, 2 vols

René Fülöp-Miller, *Die Phantasiemaschine. Eine Saga der Gewinnsucht*, Berlin: Paul Zsolnay, 1931

Urban Gad, *Der Film*, Berlin: Schuster & Loeffler, 1921

Joseph Gregor, *Das Zeitalter des Films*, Vienna and Leipzig: Reinhold, 1932

Rudolf Harms, *Philosophie des Films*, Leipzig: Felix Meiner, 1926

Nicholas Kaufmann, *Filmtechnik und Kultur*, Stuttgart and Berlin: J.G. Cotta'sche Buchhandlung Nachf., 1931

Rudolf Kurtz, *Expressionismus und Film*, Berlin: Verlag der Lichtbild-Bühne, 1926; reprint: Zurich, 1965

Konrad Lange, *Das Kino in Gegenwart und Zukunft*, Stuttgart: Ferdinand Enke, 1920

Stefan Lorant, *Wir vom Film*, Berlin: Theater- und Filmverlagsgesellschaft, 1928

Carlo Mierendorff, *Hätte ich das Kino!!*, Berlin: Erich Reiss, 1920

Curt Moreck (Konrad Haemmerling), *Sittengeschichte des Kinos*, Dresden: Paul Aretz, 1926

Kurt Mühsam and Egon Jacobsohn, *Lexikon des Films*, Berlin: Verlag der Lichtbild-Bühne, 1926

Kurt Mühsam, *Film und Kino. Ein Studien- und Berufsführer.*, Dessau: C. Dünnhaupt, 1927

Willi Münzenberg, *Erobert den Film!*, Berlin: Neuer Deutscher Verlag, 1925

László Moholy-Nagy, *Malerei, Photographie, Film*, Munich: Albert Langen, 1925; English ed.: *Painting, Photography, Film*, trans. Janet Seligman, London: Lund Humphries, 1967

Fritz Olimsky, *Tendenzen der Filmwirtschaft und deren Auswirkung auf die Filmpresse*, Berlin: Berliner Börsen-Zeitung, 1931

Wolfgang Petzet, *Verbotene Filme. Eine Streitschrift*, Frankfurt am Main: Societäts-Verlag, 1931

Hans Richter, *Filmgegner von heute – Filmfreunde von morgen*, Berlin: Hermann Reckendorf, 1929

Guido Seeber, *Der praktische Kameramann*, Berlin: Verlag der Lichtbild-Bühne, 1927; 2 vols.

Ernst Seeger, *Reichslichtspielgesetz vom 12. Mai 1920*, Berlin: C. Heymann, 1923

Fedor Stepun, *Theater und Kino*, Berlin: Bühnenvolksbund-verlag, 1932

Georg Otto Stindt, *Das Lichtspiel als Kunstform*, Bremerhaven: Atlantis, 1924

Hermann Treuner, *Filmkünstler. Wir über uns selbst*, Berlin: Sibyllen-Verlag, 1928

Curt Wesse, *Grossmacht Film, das geschöpf von kunst und technik*, Berlin: Deutsche Buchgemeinschaft, 1928

Gerhard Zaddach, *Der literarische Film*, Berlin: Deutsche Filmwoche, 1929

Hugo Zehder (ed.), *Der Film von morgen*, Berlin and Dresden: Rudolf Kaemmerer, 1923

Karl Zimmerschied, *Die deutsche Filmindustrie*, Stuttgart: C.E. Poeschel, 1922

2. Retrospective Publications

Ofer Ashkenazi, *Weimar Film and Modern Jewish Identity*, Basingstoke: Palgrave Macmillan, 2012

Rolf Aurich and Wolfgang Jacobsen (eds.), *Werkstatt Film. Selbstverständnis und Visionen von Filmleuten der zwanziger Jahre*, Munich: Edition Text + Kritik, 1998

John D. Barlow, *German Expressionist Film*, Boston: Twayne, 1982

Jürgen Berger et al. (eds.), *Erobert den Film! Proletariat und Film in der Weimarer Republik*, Berlin: Neue Gesellschaft für Bildende Kunst/Freunde der Deutschen Kinemathek, 1977

Tim Bergfelder, Sue Harris and Sarah Street, *Film Architecture and the Transnational Imagination: Set Design in 1930s European Cinema*, Amsterdam: Amsterdam University Press, 2007

Hans-Michael Bock (ed.), *The Concise Cinegraph: Encyclopaedia of German Cinema*, foreword by Kevin Brownlow, New York: Berghahn Books, 2009

Hans-Michael Bock and Michael Töteberg (eds.), *Das Ufa-Buch. Kunst und Krisen, Stars und Regisseure, Wirtschaft und Politik*, Frankfurt am Main: Zweitausendeins, 1992; 2nd ed. 1994

Hans-Michael Bock, Wolfgang Jacobsen and Jörg Schöning (eds.), *Schwarzer Traum und weisse Sklavin. Deutsch-dänische Filmbeziehungen 1910–1930*, Munich: Edition Text + Kritik, 1994

Hans-Michael Bock, Wolfgang Jacobsen and Jörg Schöning (eds.), *Fantasies russes. Russische Filmmacher in Berlin und Paris 1920–1930*, Munich: Edition Text + Kritik, 1995

Hans-Michael Bock, Wolfgang Jacobsen and Jörg Schöning

(eds.), *Geschlecht in Fesseln. Sexualität zwischen Aufklärung und Ausbeutung im Weimarer Kino 1918–1933*, Munich: Edition Text + Kritik, 2000

Ilona Brennicke and Joe Hembus, *Klassiker des Deutschen Stummfilms 1910–1930*, Munich: Goldmann, 1983

Freddy Buache, *Le cinéma allemand 1918–1933*, Renens: 5 Continents, 1984

Kenneth S. Calhoon (ed.), *Peripheral Visions: The Hidden Stages of Weimar Cinema*, Detroit: Wayne State University Press, 2001

Francis Courtade, *Cinéma Expressioniste*, Paris: Verier, 1984

Günther Dahlke and Günter Karl (eds.), *Deutsche Spielfilme von den Anfängen bis 1933. Ein Filmführer*, Berlin: Henschel, 1988–93

Lotte H. Eisner, *L'Écran demoniaque*, Paris: André Bonne, 1952; English ed.: *The Haunted Screen: Expressionism in the German Cinema and the Influence of Max Reinhardt*, trans. Roger Greaves, London: Thames & Hudson, 1969

Thomas Elsaesser, *A Second Life: German Cinema's First Decades*, Amsterdam: Amsterdam University Press, 1996

Thomas Elsaesser, *Weimar Cinema and After: Germany's Historical Imaginary*, London: Routledge, 2000

Ute Eskildsen and Jan-Christopher Horak (eds.), *Film und Foto der zwanziger Jahre. Eine Betrachtung der Internationalen Werkbundausstellung 'Film und Foto' 1929*, Stuttgart: Gert Hatje, 1979

Michael Esser (ed.), *Gleissende Schatten. Kamerapioniere der zwanziger Jahre*, Berlin: Henschel, 1994

Gero Gandert (ed.), *Der Film der Weimarer Republik. 1929. Ein Handbuch der zeitgenössischen Kritik*, Berlin and New York: de Gruyter, 1993

Ludwig Greve, Margot Pehle and Heidi Westhoff (eds.), *Hätte ich das Kino! Die Schriftsteller und der Stummfilm*, Marbach: Deutsches Literaturarchiv, 1976

Fritz Güttinger (ed.), *Der Stummfilm im Zitat der Zeit*, Frankfurt am Main: Deutsches Filmmuseum, 1984

Fritz Güttinger (ed.), *Kein Tag ohne Kino. Schriftsteller über den Stummfilm*, Frankfurt am Main: Deutsches Filmmuseum, 1984

Frank-Burkhard Habel, *Verrückt vor Begehren. Die Filmdiven der Stummfilmzeit*, Berlin: Schwarzkopf & Schwarzkopf, 1999

Sabine Hake, *The Cinema's 3rd Machine: Writings on Film in Germany 1907–1933*, Lincoln, NB, and London: University of Nebraska Press, 1993

Heinz-B. Heller, *Literarische Intelligenz und Film. Zu Veränderungen der ästhetischen Theorie und Praxis unter dem Eindruck des Films 1910–1930 in Deutschland*, Tübingen: Max Niemeyer, 1985

Knut Hickethier (ed.), *Grenzgänger zwischen Theater und Kino. Schauspielerporträts aus dem Berlin der Zwanziger Jahre*, Berlin: Verlag Ästhetik und Kommunikation, 1986

Noah Isenberg (ed.), *Weimar Cinema: An Essential Guide to Classic Films of the Era*, New York: Columbia University Press, 2009

Wolfgang Jacobsen (ed.), *Babelsberg. Das Filmstudio*, Berlin: Argon, 1992

Uli Jung and Walter Schatzberg (ed.), *Filmkultur zur Zeit der Weimarer Republik*, Munich: K.G. Saur, 1992

Anton Kaes, *Shell Shock Cinema: Weimar Culture and the Wounds of War*, Princeton, NJ, and Oxford: Princeton University Press, 2009

Oskar Kalbus, *Vom Werden deutscher Filmkunst. 1. Teil: Der stumme Film*, Altona-Bahrenfeld: Cigaretten-Bilderdienst, 1935

Laurence Kardish (ed.), *Weimar Cinema 1919–1933: Daydreams and Nightmares*, New York: Museum of Modern Art, 2010

Jürgen Kasten, *Der expressionistische Film. Abgefilmtes Theater oder avantgardistisches Erzählkino? Eine stil-, produktions- und rezeptions-geschichtliche Untersuchung*, Münster: MakS, 1991

Walter Kaul, *Schöpferische Filmarchitektur*, Berlin: Deutsche Kinemathek, 1971

Ursula von Keitz, *Im Schatten des Gesetzes. Schwangerschafts-konflikt und Reproduktion im deutschsprachigen Film 1918–1933*, Marburg: Schüren, 2005; Zürcher Filmstudien no. 13

Bernadette Kester, *Film Front Weimar: Representations of the First World War in German Films of the Weimar Period (1919–1933)*, Amsterdam: Amsterdam University Press, 2003

Christian Kiening and Heinrich Adolf (eds.), *Der absolute Film. Dokumente der Medienavantgarde (1912–1936)*, Zurich: Chronos, 2012

John Kobal, *Great Film Stills of the German Silent Era: 125 Stills from the Stiftung Deutsche Kinemathek*, introduction by Lotte H. Eisner, New York: Dover Publications, 1981

Thomas Koebner (ed.) with Norbert Grob and Bernd Kiefer, *Diesseits der 'Dämonischen Leinwand'. Neue Perspektiven auf das späte Weimarer Kino*, Munich: Edition Text + Kritik, 2003

Helmut Korte (ed.), *Film und Realität in der Weimarer Republik. Mit Analysen von Kuhle Wampe und Mutter Krausens Fahrt ins Glück*, Munich: Carl Hanser, 1978

Helmut Korte, *Der Spielfilm und das Ende der Weimarer Republik. Ein rezeptionshistorischer Versuch*, Göttingen: Vandenhoeck & Ruprecht, 1998

Siegfried Kracauer, *From Caligari to Hitler: A Psychological History of the German Film*, Princeton, NJ: Princeton University Press, 1947

Ulrike Krause, *Realität der Weimarer Republik. Gewalt und Kriminalität in deutschen Filmen der 'Goldenen Zwanziger'*, Saarbrücken: VDM Verlag Dr. Müller, 2007

Klaus Kreimeier, *The Ufa Story: A History of Germany's Greatest Film Company, 1918–1945*, trans. Robert and Rita Kimber, Berkeley, CA, and London: University of California Press, 1999

Klaus Kreimeier (ed.), *Die Metaphysik des Dekors. Raum, Architektur und Licht im klassischen deutschen Stummfilm*, Marburg: Schüren, 1994

Klaus Kreimeier, Antje Ehmann and Jeanpaul Goergen (eds.), *Geschichte des dokumentarischen Films in Deutschland*,

Sources of Quotations

Ilse Aichinger on *Liebelei*: from *Der Standard*, 23 March 2001

Michael Althen on *Pandora's Box*: from *Süddeutsche Zeitung*, 26 April 1994 ('Filmtips')

Rudolf Arnheim on *Slums of Berlin*: from *Das Stachelschwein*, no. 19, 1925

Béla Balázs on *Nosferatu*: from *Early Film Theory: Visible Man and The Spirit of Film*, Oxford and New York, 2010

Ernst Blass on *Diary of a Lost Girl*: from *Berliner Tageblatt*, 20 October 1929

Luc Bondy on *Tartuffe*: from Hans Helmut Prinzler (ed.), *Friedrich Wilhelm Murnau*, Berlin, 2003, p. 179

Thomas Brandlmeier on *The Masked Mannequin*: from Hans-Michael Bock (ed.), *CineGraph*, vol. 5, Hamburg, 1988

Heinrich Braune on *I By Day and You By Night*: from *Hamburger Echo*, 19 November 1932

Peter Buchka on *Warning Shadows*: from *Deutsche Augenblicke*, Munich, 1995, p. 22

Axel Eggebrecht on *Secrets of a Soul*: from *Die Weltbühne*, 6 April 1926

Lotte H. Eisner on *The Golem*: from *The Haunted Screen*, London, 1959, p. 66

Hans Feld on *The Love of Jeanne Ney*: from *Film-Kurier*, 8 December 1927

Bruno Frank on *Backstairs*: from *Die Weltbühne*, 15 December 1921

Rudolf Freund on *A Glass of Water*: from Günther Dahlke and Günter Karl (eds.), *Deutsche Spielfilme von den Anfängen bis 1933*, Berlin, 1988, p. 82

Fred Gehler on *The Brothers Schellenberg*: from Günther Dahlke and Günter Karl (eds.), *Deutsche Spielfilme von den Anfängen bis 1933*, Berlin, 1988, p. 126

Fritz Göttler on *From Morn to Midnight*: from Peter Buchka (ed.), *Deutsche Augenblicke*, Munich, 1995, p. 24

Frieda Grafe on *Kohlhiesel's Daughters*: from *Süddeutsche Zeitung*, 22–23 September 1979

Frieda Grafe on *Michael*: from *Süddeutsche Zeitung*, 18 January 1974 ('Filmtips')

Frieda Grafe on *Looping the Loop*: from *Cinegrafie*, no. 7, Bologna, 1990

Karola Gramann and Heide Schlüpmann on *Mädchen in Uniform*: from Hans Helmut Prinzler (ed.), *Hertha Thiele*, Berlin, 1983, p. 28

Norbert Grob on *The Street*: from Thomas Koebner (ed.), *Diesseits der 'Dämonischen Leinwand'*, Munich, 2003, pp. 64–65

Willy Haas on *The Chronicles of the Grey House*: from *Film-Kurier*, 12 February 1925

Willy Haas on *Tragedy of the Street*: from *Film-Kurier*, 16 April 1927

Michael Hanisch on *Asphalt*: from Günther Dahlke and Günter Karl (eds.), *Deutsche Spielfilme von den Anfängen bis 1933*, Berlin, 1988, p. 182

Herbert Ihering on *Variety*: from *Berliner Börsen-Courier*, 17 November 1925

Herbert Ihering on *Whither Germany?*: from *Berliner Börsen-Courier*, 1 April 1932

Anton Kaes on *Joyless Street*: Wolfgang Jacobsen, Anton Kaes and Hans Helmut Prinzler (eds.), *Geschichte des deutschen Films*, Stuttgart, 2004, pp. 57–58

Jürgen Kasten on *Homecoming*: from *Film-Bulletin*, December 1990

Alfred Kerr on *The Sins of Rose Bernd*: from *Berliner Tageblatt*, 12 February 1921

Thomas Koebner on *Hamlet*: from Erika Fischer-Lichte (ed.), *TheaterAvantgarde: Wahrnehmung, Körper, Sprache*, Tübingen, 1995, p. 111

Thomas Koebner on *Three Good Friends*: from *Diesseits der 'Dämonischen Leinwand'*, Munich, 2003, p. 355

Wolfgang Kohlhaase on *People on Sunday*: from *Auge in Auge: eine deutsche Filmgeschichte*, 2008

Siegfried Kracauer on *Ways to Strength and Beauty*: from *Frankfurter Zeitung*, 21 May 1925

Klaus Kreimeier on *The Threepenny Opera*: from Wolfgang Jacobsen (ed.), *G. W. Pabst*, Berlin, 1997, p. 57

Wilhelm Lucas Kristl on *Karl Valentin, der Sonderling*: from *Münchener Post*, 30 December 1929

Rudolf Kurtz on *Waxworks*: from *Expressionismus und Film*, Berlin, 1926, p. 79

Fritz Lang on *Woman in the Moon*: from Peter Bogdanovitch, *Fritz Lang in America*, New York, 1967, p. 20

Lichtbild-Bühne on *Anne Boleyn*: 11 December 1920

Ernst Lubitsch on *The Oyster Princess*: from a letter to Herman C. Weinberg, 10 July 1947; published in Herman C. Weinberg, *The Lubitsch Touch: A Critical Study*, New York, 1977, p. 285

Hanns G. Lustig on *The Wonderful Lies of Nina Petrovna*: from *Tempo*, 16 April 1929

B. E. Lüthge on *Madame Dubarry*: from *Film-Kurier*, 20 September 1919

Thomas Mann on *Buddenbrooks*: first published 1928; reprinted in Thomas Mann, *Gesammelte Werke* vol. X, *Reden und Aufsätze 2*, Frankfurt am Main, 1974, 2nd ed.

Corinna Müller on *Refuge*: from Hans-Michael Bock (ed.), *CineGraph*, vol. 16, Hamburg, 1990

Enno Patalas on *Destiny*: from Peter W. Jansen and Wolfram Schütte (eds.), *Fritz Lang*, Munich, 1987, p. 88

Pem (Paul Marcus) on *Congress Dances*: from Rolf Aurich and Wolfgang Jacobsen (eds.), *Pem. Der Kritiker und Feuilletonist Paul Marcus*, Munich, 2009, p. 107

Kurt Pinthus on *Dr Mabuse, the Gambler*: from *Das Tage-Buch*, 6 May 1922

Kurt Pinthus on *New Year's Eve*: from *Das Tage-Buch*, 19 January 1924

Karl Prümm on *The Last Laugh*: from Thomas Koebner (ed.), *Diesseits der 'Dämonischen Leinwand'*, Munich, 2003, p. 47

Heinz-Gerd Rasner and Reinhard Wulf on *Emil and the Detectives*: from Neil Sinyard and Adrian Turner, *Billy Wilders Filme*, Berlin, 1980, p. 415

Eric Rentschler on *The White Hell of Pitz Palü*: from Jung and Schatzberg (eds.), *Filmkultur zur Zeit der Weimarer Republik*, Munich, 1992, p. 207

Eric Rohmer on *Faust*: from *Murnaus Faustfilm*, Munich, 1980, p. 14

Rainer Rother on *The Holy Mountain*: from *Leni Riefenstahl: The Seduction of Genius*, London, 2002, p. 24

Roland Schacht (Balthasar) on *Berlin: Symphony of a Great City*: from *Das Blaue Heft*, no. 20, 15 October 1927

Werner Sudendorf on *The Blue Angel*: from *Marlene Dietrich*, Munich, 2001, p. 65

Kurt Tucholsky on *The Cabinet of Dr Caligari*: from *Die Weltbühne*, 1 March 1920

Guntram Vogt on *Berlin-Alexanderplatz*: from *Die Stadt im Kino*, Marburg, 2001, p. 258

Fritz Walter on *Mother Krausen's Journey to Happiness*: from *Berliner Börsen-Courier*, 5 January 1930

Wim Wenders on *M*: from *Auge in Auge: eine deutsche Filmgeschichte*, 2008

Sibylle Wirsing on *Doña Juana*: from Helga Belach (ed.), *Elisabeth Bergner*, Berlin, 1983, p. 32

Karsten Witte on *The Woman Men Yearn For*: from *Frankfurter Rundschau*, 20 February 1982

Hans Wollenberg on *Spies*: from *Lichtbild-Bühne*, 23 March 1928

The short texts are partially taken from *Chronik des deutschen Films* by Hans Helmut Prinzler (Stuttgart, 1995).

Index

Index